SEX, VIOLENCE and the POPES

THE LEAST PERFECT POPES IN CATHOLIC CHURCH HISTORY

By Pat Munro

PLEXNEX PRESS

Sex, Violence and the Popes

Copyright © by Pat Munro

2014

All rights reserved

ISBN-13 9781500242466

ISBN-10   1500 242 462

Sex, Violence and the Popes

Table of Contents:

CATHOLIC CHURCH ORIGINS	1
POPE VIGILIUS (537-555)	4
POPE STEPHEN III (768-772)	8
POPE LEO III (795-816)	11
POPE JOHN VIII (872-882)	15
POPE STEPHEN VI (896-897)	18
POPE SERGIUS III (904-911)	21
POPE JOHN X (914-928)	24
POPE JOHN XI (931-935)	26

POPE JOHN XII (955-964)   **28**

POPE LEO VIII (963-965)   **31**

POPE JOHN XIII (965-972)   **33**

POPE GREGORY V (996-999)   **35**

POPE SYLVESTER II (999-1003)   **38**

POPE BENEDICT IX (1032-1045)   **42**

POPE NICHOLAS II (1058-1061)   **44**

POPE GREGORY VII (1073-1085)   **46**

POPE URBAN II (1088-1099)   **49**

POPE INNOCENT III (1198-1216)   **52**

POPE GREGORY IX (1227-1241)   **59**

POPE INNOCENT IV (1243-1254)   **63**

POPE BONIFACE VIII (1293-1303)   **68**

POPE CLEMENT VI (1342-1352)   **71**

POPE URBAN VI (1378-1389)   **75**

POPE BONIFACE IX (1389-1404)   **77**

POPE PAUL II (1464-1471)   **80**

POPE SIXTUS IV (1471-1484)   **83**

POPE INNOCENT VIII (1484-1492)   **86**

POPE JULIUS II (1503-1513)   **95**

POPE LEO X (1513-1521)   **99**

POPE CLEMENT VII (1523-1534)   **103**

POPE PAUL III (1534-1549)   **107**

POPE JULIUS III (1550-1555)   **113**

POPE PAUL IV (1555-1559)   **116**

POPE PIUS V (1566-1572)   **119**

POPE URBAN VIII (1623-1644)   **122**

POPE CLEMENT XIV (1769-1774)   **128**

POPE PIUS VI (1775-1799)   **131**

POPE PIUS VII (1800-1823)   **134**

POPE LEO XII (1823-1829) **137**

POPE GREGORY XVI (1831-1846) **139**

POPE PIUS IX (1846-1878) **141**

POPE PIUS X (1903-1914) **145**

POPE PIUS XII (1939-1958) **150**

POPE JOHN PAUL I (1978) **153**

POPE BENEDICT XVI (2005-2013) **156**

THE GREAT POPES **160**

SELECTED REFERENCES: **167**

Figure 1 - Saint Peter's Crucifixion

ORIGINS OF THE CATHOLIC CHURCH

Scholars now use computers to analyze ancient writings with reliable accuracy. Their detailed textual analysis of the bible and historical cross-references provide strong evidence that Jesus really did live and did preach the Sermon on the Mount. There is also strong evidence that after he created a disturbance at the great temple in Jerusalem, Jesus was crucified by Pontius Pilate.

The true Jesus appears to have been a gifted faith healer and exorcist. He preached the imminent coming of the Kingdom of God. Some common Christian beliefs began soon after Jesus was executed, such as Jesus rising from the dead. Most bible scholars do not believe the Bible stories about the birth and childhood of Jesus are historically accurate.

By the second century after the death of Jesus, Christians also believed that their faith in Jesus would give them eternal life. A second century Roman writer named Lucian said: "These misguided creatures believe they are immortal for all times, which explains their contempt for death... it was impressed on them by their original lawgiver that they are all brothers from the moment they converted."

It is also a fact that Romans often insulted early Christians by saying Jesus was the illegitimate child of a Roman soldier. The doctrine that Jesus was born of a virgin mother did not arise until long after the death of Jesus.

Jesus told his disciples that Peter was the Rock "on which I will build my church", so Peter is considered the first Pope of the Roman Catholic Church. That might qualify him as the only Jewish pope, although he was not the only pope who had a wife. The bible is vague about Peter's fate. Church legends say had Peter was crucified upside down and buried on Vatican Hill in Rome. Saint Peter's Basilica was later built over the presumed site of Peter's grave.

In the early years Jerusalem was the center of Christianity. The church there was first led by James, the brother of Jesus. Rome was the capitol and center of the powerful Roman Empire, and over time the church in Rome became the most influential church for Christians. The first bishops of Rome tried to keep their believers united. They began to speak of the Catholic Church, meaning the universal church, which included all the separate churches following the teachings of the church in Rome.

The early leaders faced fierce persecution from Roman emperors. Roman Emperors like Caligula and Nero were extremely cruel, torturing and executing thousands of

Christians, including Saint Paul, the man who organized the Catholic Church in its earliest days. During the first 300 years of Christianity, almost every leader of the church in Rome was put to death, and thousands of other Christians were beheaded, crucified, or eaten alive by lions in the Coliseum.

Everything changed when Emperor Constantine became a Christian. He built beautiful churches and a comfortable residence for the pope. Suddenly instead of being persecuted the Christian church was actively encouraged to grow. The church flourished until Constantine moved his capitol to a newly built city far to the east. The church then split into a western church based In Rome and an eastern church based in Constantinople.

The leader of the western church in Rome became known as the 'pope', an Italian word meaning father. Pope Leo the Great reigned from 440-461 and finally established Rome's authority over other all the other churches in the west. Some of the popes who followed him were not so great...

POPE VIGILIUS (537-555)

Vigilius came from a wealthy Roman family and worked for Pope Agapitas as an ambassador to Emperor Justinian in the new capital city of Constantinople. Vigilius soon realized the real power behind the throne was the emperor's wife Theodora, an ex-actress with a tremendous appetite for sex and power. Her critics said she exhausted relays of athletes, although they didn't say it to her face.

Pope Agapitas died suddenly in 536 AD while visiting Constantinople. Theodora and Vigilius made a secret arrangement; Theodora would help him become the new pope and Vigilius would then follow directions from the empress. The empress loaded Vigilius with gold and he hurried back to Rome to bribe the voters who would choose the new pope.

Unfortunately for Vigilius, before he got back to Rome the King of the Goths had nominated his own candidate. This was Silverius, the son of a former pope. The King had a powerful army of Goths nearby, so Silverius was quickly elected. By the time Vigilius arrived back home in Rome, Pope Silverius was sitting on the papal throne. But Emperor Justinian's army soon arrived and marched into Rome. Things looked good for Vigilius until the army of Goths returned and surrounded Rome, besieging the city.

Vigilius accused Pope Silverius of planning to betray Rome by opening the city gates to the Goth army. Silverius was deposed and shipped to Constantinople. The general of Justinian's army was also getting his orders from Empress Theodora, so he appointed Vigilius as the new pope.

Emperor Justinian was a very religious man. The idea of there being two popes at the same time upset him. He sent Silverius back to Rome with orders that a fair trial be held to determine who really was the true pope.

Pope Vigilius had no interest in a fair trial. The minute Silverius arrived back in town, Vigilius had his rival arrested. After some false accusations and a brief rigged trial, Silverius was carried him off to an island prison where he was deliberately starved to death. The new pope had murdered the old pope, who had himself been the son of a pope.

Now things began to turn against Vigilius. The Emperor Justinian was trying to create a massive army so he could conquer all of Italy and add it to his empire. At the same time, the Eastern Church leaders in Constantinople were having an argument with the western church in Rome. Justinian did not want to upset his own church and create unrest at home when he was about to start a war. He ordered Vigilius to agree with the church leaders of Constantinople.

Vigilius didn't dare argue against the leaders of his own church in Rome, so he refused to support the emperor. Empress Theodora, who had provided the gold to get Vigilius elected, felt betrayed when he refused to do her bidding. While Pope Vigilius was presiding over a ceremony in church one day, the emperor's soldiers suddenly stormed in and arrested him.

The soldiers beat up the pope and put him on a ship to Constantinople. A crowd of angry Romans shouted insults and threw stones at Vigilius as he was being dragged aboard. Once back in Constantinople, Pope Vigilius changed his mind and announced he now supported the Eastern Church in their argument with Rome.

There was anger and outrage in the west, even from the pope's own supporters. Pope Vigilius was frightened and quickly reversed his position. Now he said that he did not agree with the Eastern Church after all. The emperor was not amused.

The emperor's soldiers went after Vigilius again, and the pope sought sanctuary inside a church. Pope Vigilius wrapped his arms around a pillar and hung on for dear life while the soldiers beat him and tried to drag him away by his hair and beard. The crowd in the church was appalled and chased the soldiers away.

Even the emperor was ashamed at this treatment of a pope, so he made peace with

Pope Vigilius. In return, the pope announced that in his opinion the Eastern Church was mostly but not completely correct in their argument with the western church. This decision made nobody happy. The western church was particularly angry, and they condemned their pope.

The emperor was also fed up with all this flip-flopping so he seized Pope Vigilius and put him under house arrest. The pope's closest followers were sent to prison or, even worse, sent to work in the emperor's mines. Vigilius gave up trying to please both sides and announced to everyone that he had made a mistake; he now realized the Eastern Church was completely correct.

Emperor Justinian allowed Vigilius to leave Constantinople. Pope Vigilus died on his way back to Rome, a humiliated and hated man. He is mainly remembered as the first pope to have another pope put to death so he could get the job.

POPE STEPHEN III (768-772)

Intrigue and violence surrounded the election of Pope Stephen III. Powerful Roman families were already making plans to assassinate the previous pope, Paul I, but he died before he could be murdered.

Fighting immediately broke out over who would become the next pope. The new pope would automatically become king of the Papal States as well as head of the church. Rich Roman families each pushed for their own candidates to get the job; their usual methods involved paying money to supporters and using gang violence against anyone who opposed them.

Choosing a new pope during the middle Ages almost always involved secret deals and bloody fighting in the streets of Rome. The Roman clergy who voted for popes were offered large bribes, and armed gangs threatened anyone who supported another candidate.

One wealthy Roman bishop hired a mob of soldiers to help his brother Constantine become the pope. Unfortunately for Constantine, his brother the bishop was killed by a rival gang in a street fight. Another mob seized the so-called Pope Constantine. They announced that their man Philip was the new pope. Philip actually got to sit on the pope's throne briefly, then a rival gang appeared and threw him out of the papal palace.

Finally a powerful church leader named Christopher organized the bishops and held a real election. They elected a candidate everyone thought would be easy to control. He was a monk named Stephen. He had worked for several popes but he wasn't a member of the clergy. Some people called him 'the People's Pope'. He was quickly ordained as a bishop to make him eligible to become Pope Stephen III.

The first thing Pope Stephen did was send out a gang to drag the false pope (called an 'antipope') Constantine from his hiding place. The new pope had the antipope mutilated and left him crawling along the streets of Rome with strict orders that nobody should help him in any way. After leaving his rival on the streets for a while, Pope Stephen had Constantine locked in a monastery cell where he was given another savage beating. Then his tongue was cut off and his eyes were gouged out.

Stephen's gang went on a violent spree in Rome, attacking and killing all his other rivals and their supporters. Stephen may not have personally ordered all these murderous attacks, but he made no effort to stop them.

Secret plots against the pope continued despite the violence. One of the wealthy rival families formed a private army. They disguised their soldiers as pilgrims and tried to sneak them into Rome. Pope Stephen locked the city gates to keep them out. Angry Roman mobs threatened Stephen and the rich family that supported him.

One of the pope's enemies sent a message to the people of Rome telling them to surrender, and pretended that the message had come from Stephen. His supporters began arguing among themselves. Pope Stephen's two strongest supporters were captured and blinded; one died within days and the other was locked in a dungeon and strangled to death. Stephen became ill, and his enemies took advantage of this weakness to exile or imprison all the clergy who still supported the pope.

Stephen died a few days later. Pope Stephen III was a corrupt pope whose reign is now remembered for his use of torture, mutilation, and murder to stay in power.

POPE LEO III (795-816)

Leo became pope the same day his predecessor was buried. This haste may have been to prevent the French Emperor Charlemagne from intervening with his own choice for pope.

Charlemagne had been co-ruler with his brother of a kingdom based in France. When his brother died mysteriously, Charlemagne became undisputed ruler. He was a brilliant warrior king who conquered most of Europe.

As soon as Leo was elected pope, he sent a polite letter to Charlemagne. He was thrilled to get a friendly reply, which included a large gift of money.

While Leo developed a good relationship with France, rich Romans who were relatives of the former pope hatched a plot to depose him. They decided to mutilate him so badly that he would no longer be able to perform the duties of a pope.

One day while Pope Leo was leading a procession to Mass in Rome, a gang of armed men suddenly appeared and attacked him.

They knocked him down in the street and tried to rip out his tongue and gouge out his eyes. He was left lying unconscious in the roadway, horribly mutilated. His enemies announced the news that Leo had been deposed as pope, and they had him locked away in a monastery in the countryside.

Leo managed to escape from this monastery and went to live in safety with Emperor Charlemagne's army. To everyone's surprise, he slowly recovered his sight and speech.

While he was gone his enemies spread rumors about him, accusing him of telling lies and of 'sexual misconduct'.

Charlemagne took Pope Leo back to Rome and asked the clergy to decide if the Leo was guilty. There was pretty strong evidence showing the charges against Leo actually were true.

Fortunately for the pope, witnesses were afraid to speak up, perhaps because of a church rule which forbids anyone from judging the pope. When Leo swore he was innocent of the charges, his accusers were all exiled from Rome.

On Christmas day in front of Saint Peter's tomb, Pope Leo crowned Charlemagne as Emperor of Rome, and then the pope knelt down before him.

This was a win-win arrangement; the emperor now could justify his land claims in Italy by saying he had been chosen by God, and the pope could rely on protection from the emperor's large army.

By placing the crown on the emperor's head, the pope had demonstrated to everyone that he had a role to play in the coronation of emperors. Before Charlemagne, the pope's military support came from the Emperor in Constantinople, but that eastern empire had become much weaker after years of fighting off invading Muslim armies. From now on the protection of the Catholic Church became closely tied to the most powerful Kings in Europe.

Charlemagne was also a sincere Catholic who wanted to see more Europeans join the church. His policy toward people living in the lands he conquered was simple: convert to the Catholic faith or die. When a community of Germans refused to convert from paganism he slaughtered thousands of them.

Charlemagne was the first (but not the last) king to see the value of a strong church as a uniting force for nations and empires. He also forced the Catholic Church to give its priests better training and to make church teachings the same everywhere in Europe.

Pope Leo obeyed the emperor, although he found his rules harsh. The pope spent most of his time building and decorating churches in Rome.

When Charlemagne died, some of the pope's enemies began to plot against him again. They planned to have the pope assassinated, but this time Pope Leo discovered the plot in time and had dozens of the conspirators executed.

Hundreds of years after his death, the Catholic Church decided it had been a true miracle when Leo recovered his sight and speech after the gang attacked him.

Plans were made to proclaim Pope Leo III a saint, but in 1953 his name was removed from the list - apparently there were some doubts about his holiness.

POPE JOHN VIII (872-882)

Pope John VIII was the first pope to be assassinated by his own advisors. This was a violent and dangerous era. Rome was ruled by a few wealthy families and the street gangs they supported. The street-fights were particularly nasty because the weapons used were mostly axes, hammers, clubs, and knives; only noblemen could afford proper swords.

Outside Rome, Italy was divided into feuding city-states, each with their own prince and army. Armies marched back and forth across Italy, and sometimes the fighting reached to the gates of Rome. There were also foreign invaders, ships filled with pirates, and bands of robbers lurking near the roads.

Pope John built up thick defensive walls around his property in Rome. He organized an alliance of princes to help fight off the Muslims who were invading southern Italy. The pope himself commanded a fleet of fighting ships. Soon the princes began fighting among themselves and the pope had to bribe them to keep the army together.

When the French emperor died, Pope John told the clergy to support the claims of Charles the Bald as the new emperor. Pope John then crowned Charles as emperor at

Christmas. This turned out to be a big mistake. Charles the Bald soon died, and one of the candidates the pope had rejected became the new emperor. The emperor invaded Italy, and Italian princes took advantage of Pope John's weakness to capture Rome and imprison the pope.

The pope was soon set free and ran away to hide in France. When he thought it was safe, he returned to Rome. This was another big mistake.

A group of the pope's closest advisors, probably including some of his own relatives, poisoned Pope John VIII and then beat him to death with clubs. Nobody completely understands the reasons for this murder, although one reason may have been the disgrace he brought onto the church by his deliberately feminine manners and appearance.

A strange rumor has persisted for centuries that Pope John VIII may have really been a woman, the fabled Pope Joan. There is no firm evidence that he was a woman, and most scholars are convinced the rumors are untrue. In fact, Pope Paul II was far more effeminate, often wearing make-up and elaborately jeweled costumes in public. It is true however that during his lifetime people made jokes about Pope John VIII's feminine displays, and the stories about Pope Joan became more unbelievable as time went by.

Figure 2 - The Strange Legend of 'Pope Joan'

POPE STEPHEN VI (896-897)

Pope Stephen VI was a man consumed by fanatical hatred. It is the reason he is remembered as an evil pope who was probably insane. It is also the reason he died so soon after being elected pope.

There were three popes during the year Stephen was elected pope. Old Pope Formosus had died first. His replacement Pope Boniface VI died a few days after being elected; Pope Boniface is remembered as the only man elected pope after twice being defrocked for immoral behavior. Then it was Stephen's turn.

Pope Stephen VI had always hated Pope Formosus. They had been bitter political enemies, and Stephen was furious when Formosus defeated him and was elected as pope. Formosus had another powerful enemy, Holy Roman Emperor Lambert. The Holy Roman empire was made up of several European nations that followed the Catholic faith, and whoever was crowned as their emperor was sure to become a very rich and powerful man.

When Pope Formosus was first elected he had crowned Lambert as the new holy Roman Emperor, but later on he also crowned another nobleman as co-emperor.

The new co-emperor died very suddenly, and Emperor Lambert urged Pope Stephen to take revenge on their common enemy. The only problem was that Pope Formosus had been dead for several months before Stephen became pope.

The result was one of the most disgusting events in the history of the church; it became known as the Cadaver Synod. Stephen called a meeting of bishops (a "synod") to put Formosus on trial. The dead pope was charged with perjury and violating church laws. Pope Stephen ordered his men to dig up the decaying corpse of Pope Formosus and take it from its tomb. The rotting corpse was dressed in papal robes and propped up on a throne. Then Stephen began the macabre trial.

A deacon was appointed to speak for the dead pope, and Pope Stephen acted as prosecutor. He shouted at the corpse as if it was alive. While the gruesome trial was underway, an earthquake rocked Rome and badly damaged the Lateran Basilica, the pope's own cathedral church.

At the end of this strange trial, Pope Stephen declared the dead pope guilty. He had his men strip the putrefying body and mutilate it by hacking off three fingers on its right hand - the fingers that popes use to give blessings and swear oaths. They buried the corpse again, but soon after Stephen changed his mind and had the body dug up again. This time he ordered that it be thrown into the Tiber River.

Figure 3 - Pope Stephen and the Cadaver Synod

The scandal that resulted from this trial led to Pope Stephen's downfall. Stories began to spread that the body of Pope Formosus had appeared on the banks of the Tiber and was performing miracles.

There was a widespread uprising against Pope Stephen, and barely a year after his election a mob threw him in prison, where he was strangled to death.

POPE SERGIUS III (904-911)

Sergius came from one of the rich families in Rome that constantly fought with each other over who would become the next pope.

It is almost surprising that anyone wanted to become pope during the middle ages. Popes lived in constant danger of being murdered or deposed by their rivals. What made the job so attractive was the power and wealth of the position. The pope appointed cardinals, bishops, and other senior members of the church, and the pope also collected vast sums of money from his lands and from the churches all over Europe. It was usual in rich families for the oldest son to take over the family business from his father, and for the second oldest son to obtain a senior position in the church (often by paying a bribe). There was constant rivalry among the senior clergy to move higher, perhaps even becoming the pope someday.

One eager rival named Christopher had his gang seize the current Pope Leo V and lock him in a prison. But antipope Christopher did not have enough support to hold on to the job, and the Roman clergy held an election and chose Sergius as their new pope.

Sergius was also quickly removed, this time by the Holy Roman emperor who named his own choice as Pope John IX. Pope John's first act was to ex-communicate Sergius and his followers, and Sergius had to flee from Rome and live in exile.

Seven years later the antipope Christopher's gang seized Pope John and threw him in prison. The rich family that had arranged the election of Sergius now convinced him to return to Rome. They organized their own group of armed fighters and seized antipope Christopher, throwing him into prison.

Pope Sergius III determined to make sure his rivals did not throw him into prison. The first thing he did when he began his reign was to have both Pope John IX and antipope Christopher strangled to death in their prisons. He then appointed the men who helped him into the most powerful positions in the Roman Catholic Church.

Like many popes, Sergius was really a puppet of the Roman families that had put him in power. Sergius had to threaten his clergy with violence to make them support the results of the eerie Cadaver Synod. There was little public outcry this time since Sergius and his allies controlled the local military in Rome.

There is strong evidence that Pope Sergius had an affair with a fifteen year-old girl named Marozia. She was the daughter of the Count of Tusculum, head of the rich and powerful family that was the pope's strongest supporter. Marozia and Sergius had a child together who later became Pope John XI.

Marozia herself became very rich, and she developed a lot of influence over papal affairs. Later historians often refer to the reign of Pope Sergius III as the beginning of a sixty-year 'pornocracy', which is sometimes also called 'the rule of harlots'.

Sergius III died after seven stormy years as pope. He remains the only pope known to have fathered an illegitimate son who then went on to become pope himself. When Pope Sergius died, the church leaders decided not to preserve his tomb because of the shame he had brought on the church.

POPE JOHN X (914-928)

John was a bishop who rose to power after meeting Theodora, wife of the powerful Count of Tusculum. They became lovers during his time in Rome, although it was said they were related to each other. With Theodora's support, John was soon promoted to Archbishop. When Pope Lando died, John was crowned as Pope John X without bothering to hold an election.

The rich families who controlled Rome wanted a strong pope who could lead resistance to Saracen raiders. These Muslim warriors had established a base in Italy and were looting the countryside. Pope John X organized a coalition of Italian princes and the pope himself led their combined armies into battle. Along with his ally King Berengar, the pope was able to win a great victory over the Muslims.

John hoped that together they could unite the city-states of Italy into a single powerful nation, but instead a group of jealous Italian princes assassinated Berengar. The Count of Tusculum died soon after; he had been head of the rich family that had always been John's best supporter. With his two most powerful allies dead, Pope John was suddenly in a very dangerous situation.

As John's power had grown he had begun acting more independently, refusing to obey suggestions from the wealthy Roman families. Theodora had a daughter named Marozia, and she became angry with the Pope John's unwillingness to do what he was told. She began to plot against the disobedient pope.

Marozia and her husband decided to attack Pope John's favorite brother Peter. Pope John had made his brother a duke, but now Duke Peter was threatened and forced to flee his dukedom. The pope was upset and helped Peter collect a small army and return to Rome with it. Marozia and her husband decided to leave him alone. Instead, they began to secretly build up their own army.

When the time was ripe, the forces of Marozia made a surprise attack on the pope's palace. The pope watched as his brother Peter was cut into pieces before his eyes, and then Pope John himself was thrown into prison.

Pope John X was strangled to death in his prison cell, almost certainly by killers sent by Marozia. Marozia herself became the ruler of Rome and appointed the next three popes. The third one was the illegitimate son she had with Pope Sergius III.

POPE JOHN XI (931-935)

Pope John XI was about twenty years old when he was elected. His mother Marozia was the ruler of Rome, and his father was Pope Sergius III. He appears to be the only illegitimate son of a pope who later became pope himself.

He did what his mother told him, even taking part in Marozia's wedding to her own brother-in-law. Since her groom was already married, the pope had agreed to grant a divorce. This violated church law, and Marozia's son Alberic led a revolt against her and his half-brother.

Alberic led an angry mob and stormed into her castle in the middle of the wedding ceremony. Marozia and Pope John XI were seized; her new husband ran away and escaped with his life. Alberic announced that he was now the Prince of Rome, and he locked his mother and his half-brother (the pope) in prison.

Alberic later released the pope but kept him under house arrest in Rome. It is said he treated Pope John as his slave, and John XI died as a powerless pawn in a family power struggle.

Marozia was never heard of again. It is said Alberic kept his mother locked up until she died fifty years later. She had an astonishing effect on the history of the Catholic Church.

As historian Edward Gibbon puts it:
"The bastard son, the grandson, the great grandson, and two great-great grandsons of Marozia — a rare genealogy — was seated in the Chair of Saint Peter."

Her son Alberic, the 'Prince of Rome', never became pope, but her grandson Octavian later became Pope John XII.

POPE JOHN XII (955-964)

Octavian was the grandson of Marozia and the son of Alberic II, the self-styled Prince of Rome. Octavian's mother may have been Alberic's step-sister, or perhaps one of his concubines. They were all members of the most powerful family in Rome.

When Alberic died, Octavian became the new Prince of Rome, and the following year he was crowned as Pope John XII. He was about eighteen years old, very young for a pope Like many teenagers, John paid far more attention to being prince than he did to being pope. Church affairs held little interest for him; he much preferred to chasing women, drinking, gambling, and hunting.

John XII did lead an army against Italian dukes who had seized some of his papal lands, but his army's efforts were unsuccessful. The King of Italy then attacked the pope's lands. Pope John asked King Otto of Germany to come and help him. King Otto agreed, and in return John crowned Otto as the Holy Roman Emperor.

When he met John XII, King Otto observed that the pope "passed his whole life in vanity and adultery". He suggested to Pope John that he should change his wild ways, but the pope ignored this advice. King Otto led the German army against the King of Italy and defeated him. Then Otto's army marched toward Rome.

The Romans split into two camps; one group supported Pope John, and one supported their new Emperor Otto. Pope John put on his armor and led his army against Otto. When the armies got near each other, John was frightened and decided he could not win the battle. Instead of fighting, he packed up the papal treasury and escaped from Rome.

When John XII refused to return, Otto named Leo VIII as the new pope. Pope John XII was condemned for being immoral and depraved, and was accused of turning the pope's palace into a brothel.

Pope John's Roman supporters revolted against Leo, and many of them were slaughtered. John himself did not join the fight; instead he went off on a long hunting party in the mountains. He waited until Otto left Rome and took his army back to Germany. Then John XII returned to Rome with his own army.

The pope had some of his opponents tortured and mutilated, and the remainder quickly agreed to support him. Pope John XII ruled again as pope Prince of Rome until his sudden death at the age of twenty-eight. It was said Pope John XII died of a heart attack or stroke while in bed with a married woman. Many Romans did not think it was a heart attack; they believed it was the jealous husband who killed the pope.

Figure 4 - Emperor Otto I meets Pope John XII

POPE LEO VIII (963-965)

When Emperor Otto marched into Rome to depose the young and lusty Pope John XII, that pope had already emptied the Vatican treasury and fled into the countryside. The Emperor announced that John XII was no longer the true pope, and he nominated a man named Leo as his choice to be the new pope. But there was a problem.

Leo was a school superintendent in Rome. That meant he was a layman, not an ordained member of the church, so he was not eligible to become pope. The emperor's candidate was rapidly promoted. In a single day Leo was ordained as a priest and then promoted to Bishop of Rome. Then he was crowned as Pope Leo VIII, reigning at the same time as John XII.

Leo VIII belonged to a powerful Roman family, but there were many people in Rome who didn't like taking orders from a puppet of the German emperor. Pope John was hiding in the countryside, but his agents paid bribes to the powerful Roman families and their supporters took to the streets in revolt.

Otto's soldiers quickly crushed the revolt with considerable slaughter. Leo VIII was a merciful pope, and he convinced Otto not to execute the hostages taken from Rome's most powerful families. The pope believed after his act of kindness these families would become friendly to him. But as soon as Emperor Otto and his army left Rome and marched back to Germany, the Romans revolted again. Pope Leo was forced to flee to the safety of Emperor Otto's court.

Pope John XII returned to Rome and organized a meeting of clergy; they deposed Leo VIII and declared he was an antipope. Then John XII died suddenly in bed with a married woman), and the Romans quickly chose a new pope named Benedict V.

An angry Emperor Otto returned from Germany with his army and attacked Rome. Soon Leo VIII once again sat on the papal throne. This time he called for a meeting at the pope's palace with the Roman clergy.

They agreed to depose Pope Benedict, but Leo showed mercy to his rival Benedict. Instead of having him put to death, he was exiled to Germany. Perhaps Leo had sympathy for his rival because he knew what it felt like to be deposed.

Pope Leo VIII died soon after. There is still a religious debate whether Leo was a true pope or just another antipope. In fact, he was both.

POPE JOHN XIII (965-972)

The father of Pope John XIII was a rich Roman nobleman who was also a bishop. John grew up inside the pope's Lateran Palace in Rome. When Pope Leo VIII died, John the bishop was identified as someone who might be acceptable both to the Roman people and to the German Emperor Otto. He was elected as Pope John XIII by a unanimous vote.

Pope John immediately gave members of his own family the most powerful positions in the church; this was common practice for newly elected popes and was done in order to fill the Roman clergy with loyal supporters. But support from the local clergy was not all a pope needed to feel safe in his position. Pope John's troubles began when Emperor Otto and his army went home to Germany. Several Italian princes began to raise their own armies, and wealthy families in Rome organized a revolt against the new pope.

Within a few weeks of being elected, Pope John was assaulted, beaten up, thrown into prison, and then sent into exile.

The exiled pope was able to send a message to the emperor letting him know what had happened. Emperor Otto turned around and marched his army back to Rome. Now the supporters of Pope John XIII rose up, murdering John's enemies and recapturing the city.

The Roman people appeared happy to welcome John back as their pope, but the Emperor Otto was not impressed. He was so furious with the treachery of the Romans that showed little mercy to the leaders of their revolt. Many of them were hung from the city walls; others were blinded. Pope John was so grateful he called Otto 'a three-time blessed emperor.'

The pope continued to take very good care of his own family. He even gave his sister her own town. There were no more revolts during the rest of his reign, but when Pope John XIII died he was buried outside the walls of Saint Paul's Basilica.

POPE GREGORY V (996-999)

Gregory V was the first German pope. His real name was Bruno, and he was a cousin of the new Emperor, Otto III. Bruno was crowned as Pope Gregory V when he was just twenty-four years old. It is not certain that he really wanted the job. This isn't surprising when one considers what happened to the popes who had reigned before him.

Beginning with Pope John XII's sudden death in bed, a series of popes had experienced untimely endings to their reigns. Pope Benedict V had been besieged and deposed. Pope Leo VIII had been exiled, deposed, and ex-communicated.

Pope Benedict VI had been imprisoned and strangled to death, Pope John XIV was imprisoned and starved to death, and Pope John XV lived only a few months before dying of fever. That is when Emperor Otto III gave the job to young Bruno.

Pope Gregory's first duty was to officially crown his cousin as Emperor Otto III. Then Gregory decided to please the powerful Roman families by making decisions he knew they would approve – the new pope they had a history of using money and violence to replace popes they didn't like.

Gregory convinced the emperor to pardon some of the rich Roman noblemen who had been involved in the revolt against Pope John XIII. Before long, Gregory even began to make his own decisions without consulting his cousin Otto III, the new German Emperor.

This upset the emperor, who then refused to honor an agreement to return some conquered lands to the Papal States. The Papal States were ruled by the pope as his own kingdom, and the size of his states was a big factor in determining the pope's annual income. The grumpy emperor and his soldiers left Rome in June, and Pope Gregory immediately had a rival.

This was Crescentius, one of the men Pope Gregory had asked the emperor to pardon instead of sending him into exile for his revolt against Pope John XV. Now this traitor organized the noblemen of Rome and led a rebellious mob that chased Gregory out of town. The wealthy Roman families then elected their own pope, John XVI, who became the antipope.

Twice Gregory V and his supporters tried to recapture Rome but both times they failed. Then Emperor Otto III marched his army toward Rome and the antipope ran away. The emperor's soldiers captured him and sliced off his nose and ears, cut out his tongue, and blinded him. He was publicly humiliated, and then Pope Gregory had him locked up in a German monastery where he lived out the rest of his days.

Crescentius, the nobleman who led the uprising, locked himself inside a castle. The emperor's troops stormed the castle and captured the traitor. He was beheaded, and his body hung from the castle walls.

Gregory V was back on the pope's throne, no doubt a less trusting young man than he had been a year earlier. He died suddenly at the age of thirty. A sudden attack of malaria was given as the cause. Foul play was suspected, but has never been proved.

POPE SYLVESTER II (999-1003)

Gerbert d'Aurillac was born in France and became a monk while he was in his teens. He was an excellent student of science and mathematics. When he visited Rome he met Pope John XIII and the German Emperor Otto. The young man's knowledge impressed the pope, and he convinced the emperor to hire Gerbert as tutor to the emperor's son, who became Emperor Otto III.

When Gregory V died, the emperor helped get his former tutor elected as pope. Gerbert chose the name Pope Sylvester II. His reign coincided with a happy period of global warming in Europe. During this 'Little Warm Age' crops and animals thrived and life was easier for everyone, even the peasants. By the time this warming ended in 1300, the population in Europe almost doubled.

Although Pope Sylvester was well-educated and a strong leader of the church, he was also a Frenchman and the people in Rome did not enjoy having a foreigner on the papal throne. Sylvester didn't win any friends by working hard to stop the clergy from taking bribes and keeping concubines.

Pope Sylvester didn't believe that being from a wealthy noble family qualified someone to become a bishop. He said he would only appoint bishops if they were competent men who led moral lives. The Romans revolted, and Pope Sylvester was forced to flee for his life. The new emperor Otto III tried twice to recapture Rome but he failed. He died during his third attempt.

Sylvester II eventually returned, but the wealthy families now controlled the city. The pope died very soon after his return.

Many strange stories were told about Pope Sylvester II and his mysterious powers. While he was alive, his enemies had spread rumors that Sylvester was an evil sorcerer in league with the devil. They said a female demon had helped him become pope. Another story said he had won the pope's job by playing dice with the devil. The pope was even accused of creating a magic robotic head that could answer 'yes' or 'no' to his questions.

It was also said that if Sylvester ever read a mass in Jerusalem the devil would appear and seize him. The pope, it was said, cancelled a planned trip to Jerusalem, but later after reading a mass in a church called The Holy Cross of Jerusalem he became very ill.

While he was dying he is supposed to have asked his cardinals to cut him up and spread the pieces of his body around the city of Rome. In another one of these frightening stories, the devil had actually attacked Pope Sylvester while he was reading a mass in church; the devil gouged-out the pope's eyes and gave them to little demons to play with.

The real truth is that during the years he lived in Spain, Gerhart had studied with Arab teachers. When he returned, he brought back advanced ideas and inventions unknown in Europe in the Middle Ages. What appeared to the uneducated as magic powers were really the products of his superior knowledge of science and algebra. He used an abacus to solve mathematical problems nobody else could, and an astrolabe to predict the movements of the stars.

Figure 5 - Pope Sylvester II... and the Devil

POPE BENEDICT IX (1032-1045)

Benedict was about twenty years old when he became Pope, one of the youngest Popes in history. His rich father had to pay a lot of bribes to get young Benedict the job, especially since Benedict had no training or experience.

He was a wild young man, debauched and violent. People accused him of holding homosexual orgies in the Pope's Lateran Palace. Even the tough Roman crowd couldn't stand him, and they threw him out of Rome in 1044. The mob appointed a bishop as Pope Sylvester III. Benedict returned with a private army and after bloody street-fighting in Rome, Benedict IX was back on the papal throne again.

Pope Benedict was accused of rapes, murders, and other crimes, and once again the crowd forced him to leave Rome. They restored Pope Sylvester III to the papal palace. But Benedict soon returned with his private army and chased Sylvester out of town.

It cost a lot of money to pay for a private army, and Benedict was soon short of money. He was also thinking about getting married, so he sold his position as pope to his Godfather in exchange for a large cash payment. The Godfather named himself Pope Gregory VI. The first thing Pope

Gregory did was give lots of cash to the Roman mobs to keep them on his side.

After living in the countryside for a while, Benedict got bored with his retirement and returned to Rome. He claimed that he was still the real Pope, and his fighting men took over the city. Pope Gregory fled, still claiming that he was the true Pope. Then Sylvester reappeared on the scene and announced that in fact he really was the only true Pope.

This was way too much confusion for the very religious King Henry of Germany. He arrived in Rome to be crowned by the Pope and found there were three Popes there, each one claiming to be the true pope and all of them fighting with each other. King Henry held a meeting of bishops, and all three Popes were 'fired'.

Benedict's private army captured the Pope's palace, but then German troops chased him out. A German Pope was elected, and he ex-communicated Benedict for taking bribes. Benedict left Rome and settled into a comfortable life in the Italian countryside, where he died peacefully seven years later.

Pope Benedict IX was the only man to become Pope more than once; he was actually the pope on three separate occasions. He is also the only Pope who is known to have sold his position as Pope to someone else.

POPE NICHOLAS II (1058-1061)

Pope Stephen IX had worked hard to reform the church, and as he lay dying he made the cardinals promise not to elect a new pope until the leader of the reformers returned from Germany. He wanted them to complete the work he had been doing to make all clergy follow church rules more closely. While the reformers waited, the anti-reformers among the rich Roman families went ahead and elected their own pope, who took the name Benedict X.

The cardinals in favor of reforms complained that bribes had been paid to get Benedict elected. Violent gangs then forced them o flee from Rome. These cardinals met separately and elected a Frenchman who became Pope Nicholas II.

Pope Nicholas returned to Rome with a French army, and Pope Benedict ran away. Nicholas and his French knights chased Benedict and after several battles they forced him to surrender his claim to the Papal throne.

Nicholas II paid for this French support by giving them lands in Italy, including Sicily. The land wasn't really his to give away, but he used a forged letter as proof that the land belonged to the church. With the French army backing him, Nicholas was able to convince the bishops to agree on changes to how popes were chosen.

The usual way a new pope was chosen depended on a handful of rich Roman families. New popes were usually nominated by the strongest local gang, by whoever paid the largest bribes, or by an Emperor with a threatening army. Sometimes the local clergy would assemble and vote, and other times people would simply shout out the name of their preferred choice for new pope at the funeral for the old pope.

Nicholas tried to clean up this system. After Nicholas II, popes were to be elected at a meeting of cardinals in Rome. There would still be some role for emperors to influence elections, but they would not have the absolute right to choose new popes. At least that was the theory. Nicholas II sent a cardinal to explain the new rules, but the German emperor was so upset he refused to meet with the cardinal.

After Nicholas died, the cardinals followed the new rules. They met together and elected Pope Alexander II. But the rich Roman families had support from the German emperor and ignored the new election rules. They named Honorius as the true Pope. But Pope Alexander II called for help, and French troops threw Honorius out of Rome.

POPE GREGORY VII (1073-1085)

When Pope Alexander II died, a commotion arose at his funeral as people shouted out Gregory's name as their choice for Pope. The cardinals met the same day and elected him as Pope Gregory VII. Some people found this very suspicious and wondered if the funeral crowd had been bribed.

More worrisome for Gregory VII was the fact that nobody had consulted the German emperor about who should become the new Pope. Luckily for Pope Gregory, Emperor Henry IV was still very young and had troubles at home. This was no time for him to fight with the church, so he promised to support the pope.

Pope Gregory had never been a priest or bishop, but he had been a papal administrator and knew how the system worked. He held a council where he announced that from now on only the pope could appoint, relocate or depose bishops. He also claimed that: "the pope has never erred... and never will err to all eternity."

Emperor Henry IV finally defeated the troublesome German rebels and turned his attention toward Italy. The emperor claimed northern Italy as part of his empire, and to prove his power he named a new archbishop in the northern city of Milan.

Pope Gregory replied with a letter accusing the German Emperor of treachery, and saying that perhaps the emperor should lose his crown for trying to cancel the pope's decision. This made Emperor Henry furious. He gathered together the German bishops and they declared Pope Gregory deposed.

The pope responded by ex-communicating the emperor. This was a real showdown to see who had more power. Did the emperor have the power to remove a pope, or did the pope have the power to have an emperor removed? It turned out that most of the people in Germany supported the church, and once again Emperor Henry's army had to battle rebels at home.

Pope Gregory VII made Emperor Henry IV beg for forgiveness, and made him make new promises to support the pope. However when the rebels actually defeated the Emperor in a battle, the pope announced that he was once again ex-communicating the Emperor.

This time most people felt the pope's decision was wrong. Then the leader of the rebels died, and suddenly the Emperor had regained control of his whole empire. He was older and wiser now, and he marched his army into Rome and named a friend of his as Pope Clement III.

Pope Gregory was able to escape from Rome with the help of a French army - which looted Rome while it was there. Pope Gregory VII died in exile a year later.

His foes said he was guilty of ordering tortures, assassinations and executions without trials. His supporters praised him for reforming the church law governing election of popes, and for strengthening the role of the pope as supreme leader of the church.

Seven hundred years later Pope Benedict XIII canonized him as Saint Gregory.

Figure 6 - Emperor Henry IV forced to beg forgiveness from Pope Gregory VII

POPE URBAN II (1088-1099)

Urban II was a French pope who launched a European crusade to capture Holy Lands for Christians.

Muslim armies had captured Jerusalem and Palestine in 636. They continued to expand their empire and by 1071 almost all of the Byzantine Empire was in Muslim hands. All that remained under Christian control was the capitol Constantinople and the land that surrounded it. In 1074 Byzantine Emperor Alexios asked the west for military help.

Pope Urban II called a meeting of bishops and feudal lords in Clermont, France. The pope urged western Christians to come to the aid of the Byzantine Empire, telling them it was God's will. A general call went out to all the knights and nobles of France.

The pope's speech was very successful in convincing people to go on a holy war against the Muslims. A hundred thousand soldiers volunteered. When they agreed to join the crusade, the pope promised them that God would not punish their sins. Crusaders from all over Western Europe served under various feudal commanders.

The crusade got off to a bad start. A preacher named Peter the Hermit raised an army of 20,000 peasants and headed for the Holy Lands in 1096. The peasants were ambushed by a Muslim army in Turkey and almost all of them were slaughtered or sold into slavery.

The army of French Crusaders marched south and on their way to the Muslim lands they attacked and killed thousands of Jews; some accounts say hundreds of thousands. They called themselves the Knights of Christ.

In 1097 the Crusader armies reached Turkey and surrounded the Muslim city of Antioch. After a long siege the city was betrayed by one of its Christian inhabitants. Once the crusaders got inside the walls they massacred all the Muslims and looted the city. A large Muslim army arrived too late to save Antioch, and it was also defeated by the crusaders. Instead of handing the captured city back to the Byzantines as they had promised, the leaders of the crusading army decided to keep Antioch for themselves.

The leaders were happy to stay there, but their soldiers revolted and insisted they march on toward Jerusalem. The Muslim Shiites had just captured Jerusalem from the Turkish Muslims and they believed the crusaders would stay in Turkey. They were shocked in June 1099 when a huge crusader army appeared outside their walls.

The Jews and Muslims inside the city joined together to keep the crusaders out. They threw out the Christian inhabitants fearing they might betray the city. After five weeks of fighting the crusaders got inside the city walls; they looted the city and destroyed its mosques. When a large Muslim army approached, the crusaders murdered all the Jews and Muslims inside Jerusalem.

The heavy armor worn by the Christian knights made them very difficult to kill. The Muslim army was defeated and fled. The crusaders now held a strip of land stretching from Antioch in Turkey to Jerusalem in the Holy Lands. This was a large empire containing rich cities, so many crusaders decided to settle down as rulers of their newly conquered lands. They built enormous castles that still dominate the landscape today.

Some of the fiercest crusaders were the Knights Templar, warrior monks who later became immensely wealthy. They built churches where they displayed relics from the Holy Land. They even set up their own banking system.

Pope Urban II died two weeks after his crusading army captured Jerusalem. He died before the news reached Rome.

In 1881 Pope Urban II was declared a saint.

POPE INNOCENT III (1198-1216)

Innocent III was one of nine popes who came from the wealthy Conti family. He had been a lawyer, and was described as "a small, handsome, and very energetic man." He was 37 when elected Pope.

Later that year he was appointed as the guardian of Prince Frederick II, the four year-old heir to the Holy Roman Empire. Pope Innocent confirmed little Frederick as King of Sicily and later convinced the young king to marry the widow of the King of Hungary.

Innocent used his power over the bishops to strengthen the position of pope as the universal authority in Europe. He gained greater influence for the popes in the selection of kings by offering church support to the pope's preferred candidates in royal succession disputes.

The pope slowly began to regain papal lands (and incomes) that had been lost over the years. Pope Innocent III became widely acknowledged as the most powerful man in Europe.

Innocent announced that although princes had the right to elect their own king, the pope had the power to decide if their choice was worthy. If the pope decided their choice was unworthy then the princes would have to choose somebody else as king. After a lengthy dispute, most European kings acknowledged the pope's authority.

Innocent III declared a war on heresy and condemned anyone who rejected the teachings of the Catholic Church. When one of his representatives was murdered in southern France, Pope Innocent asked the King of France to suppress heretics there. These were communities of Christians like the Cathars, who claimed to be Catholics but did not agree with everything the pope said.

This resulted in the slaughter of about 20,000 men, women, and children, many of whom were Catholics.

Figure 7 - Expulsion of Cathars

Pope Innocent also started a new crusade with the aim of recapturing Jerusalem and the Holy Lands. Jerusalem had been lost in 1187 when the brilliant Muslim leader Saladin trapped the crusader army in the desert outside the city; most of the European knights died of thirst or were roasted alive inside their heavy armor.

A legend became common that a Children's Crusade took place to rescue Jerusalem from the Muslims. One version says a boy was visited by Jesus and told to lead a peaceful crusade of children to convert the Muslims to Christianity. The boy performed enough 'miracles' to convince thousands of children to follow him toward the Holy Lands. Alas, the children who did board ships for Jerusalem were instead taken to North Africa and sold into slavery.

Modern scholars believe the legend of the Children's Crusade has become wildly exaggerated over the years. It appears more likely that the 'children' were actually teenage boys, much like the boy-soldiers still being recruited in Africa today.

Pope Innocent negotiated a peace between France and England so both would be free to send knights to help with his new crusade. Many French knights and nobles joined him, but the English were reluctant. In the end, most of the men in the Fourth Crusade were French.

To pay for this crusade, the pope greatly increased taxes on his subjects, but collecting the taxes proved to be difficult. Then the pope announced that anyone who had promised to join the Crusade could pay him cash to be released from their vow. He also offered an indulgence to ease the punishment of sins for anyone who joined the crusade or who contributed money to support it.

The Fourth Crusade went sideways. There was less enthusiasm than before for crusading, and this new army didn't have enough money to buy supplies or pay for ships to carry them to the Holy Lands.

The French crusaders made a deal with the Republic of Venice to pay for ships to take them to Egypt, but when they reached Venice the crusaders could not pay their bill. Things rapidly spun out of control.

Venice agreed to carry the crusaders to the nearby Christian city of Zara so they could loot it and pay their debt. Pope Innocent had forbidden any attacks on Christian cities, but the crusaders ignored him. The crusaders made a surprise attack on Zara, looting everything they could carry away and killing anyone who tried to stop them.

The pope was shocked and ex-communicated the crusaders, but he soon forgave them in exchange for their promise to continue his crusade to rescue Jerusalem. Once the crusaders were aboard their ships, their leaders decided instead that it would be far more profitable to attack and loot Constantinople, the immensely wealthy Christian capitol of Byzantium. The ancient capital of the Eastern Church was completely looted, with much of the booty taken back to Venice.

Although Innocent III did not order the attack, he quickly realized that the capture of Constantinople might give him a way to rejoin the eastern and western churches. For the next sixty years Constantinople was under Roman control.

Pope Innocent's greatest accomplishment was organizing the Fourth Lateran Council in 1215. Over a thousand religious leaders from all over Europe attended. They made practical reforms to the church such as establishing schools, preaching in the language of the people instead of ancient Latin, and making consistent rules for confessions and communions. They also agreed on a definition of the holy trinity and confirmed the miracle of transubstantiation (the exact moment at Mass when the bread and wine suddenly changes into the actual flesh and blood of Christ).

The Council also ordered harsher persecution of Jews, and it made plans for a Fifth Crusade to be launched in 1217. Pope Innocent III, however, died suddenly in 1216, apparently of a violent fever.

The mysterious circumstances surrounding his death have never been explained. One evening his body was found lying naked on the floor of a cathedral. It appears he had been robbed and abandoned by all including his own servants. Pope Innocent III left the Catholic Church near the peak of its power.

Figure 8 - The Crusaders Attacking Constantinople

POPE GREGORY IX (1227-1241)

Ugolino da Segni was a nephew of Pope Innocent III. When he became Pope Gregory IX his priority was to tighten up church law and crack down on those who weren't following his orders. He published a collection of papal letters to list all decisions about church law in one place. This remained the standard guide to church law until the 20th century.

The new pope reopened the University of Paris and started a new university in Toulouse, and he relaxed the ban on reading the works of Aristotle. But these progressive actions are not what made the reign of Pope Gregory IX so memorable.

Pope Gregory also created the Papal Inquisition, and made death an acceptable punishment for those who did not follow the teachings of the church. He authorized the church to use force to correct 'errors' in what people believed and what they did. The instrument he developed to correct these errors was the Inquisition.

Gregory started by attacking groups of German Catholics who were not following Roman orders closely enough. Dominican friars were the most relentless participants the Inquisition; they became known as 'the Hounds of the Lord.' Gregory had a particular hatred for Jews. He condemned them to 'perpetual servitude' and had thousands of their holy books confiscated and burned.

A century later when the Black Death swept across Europe, some people blamed Pope Gregory's Inquisition for making the death toll worse. It was said a shortage of cats in Europe allowed rats to breed and spread the plague. Although Gregory had never ordered a cat massacre, cats were commonly believed to be used in devil worship and people afraid of the Inquisition may have killed their cats, just to be safe from suspicion.

Pope Gregory ex-communicated German Emperor Frederick II for failing to keep his promise to lead a sixth crusade into the Holy Lands. The following year Frederick and his army did leave Europe and invade the Holy Land, where they defeated the Muslim armies, and recaptured Jerusalem. But while they were gone, Pope Gregory created an army to seize some of Frederick's territory. Frederick hurried back and easily defeated the pope's army. The Roman people were upset and revolted against Gregory, forcing him to leave Rome.

The pope made peace with Emperor Frederick, but it didn't last and soon war between the pope and the emperor broke out again. Gregory called a council and summoned bishops from all over Europe to Rome. Frederick sent out his navy to see if he could capture or drown some of the bishops travelling by sea to Rome for the big meeting. His ships actually captured and kidnapped almost 100 bishops.

Some of these bishops turned against Gregory. A German Archbishop called him the Antichrist and accused the pope of bragging: "I am God, I cannot err."

By August the emperor's army had surrounded Rome, but Gregory IX died before the emperor could capture him.

Figure 9 - The Inquisition Searching for Heretics

POPE INNOCENT IV (1243-1254)

When Pope Gregory died, the cardinals met to choose the next pope, they followed new church rules that required two thirds of the cardinals to agree. This proved difficult.

German Emperor Frederick II ordered his soldiers to keep the cardinals locked inside a leaky old building and would not let them out until they made a choice.

Conditions were extremely unpleasant; there were even guards stationed on the roof, and it is said their urine dripped down onto the miserable cardinals inside. It was so hot and unsanitary that one cardinal died.

The desperate cardinals finally agreed to choose an old feeble man as pope. They knew he would die soon, but in the meantime they would be free to work out their choice for the pope who would come next.

In fact the new Pope did die just seventeen days later, and the terrified cardinals ran away from Rome to avoid meeting again so soon. It took two years before the cardinals could all be gathered together again. This time they elected Sinibaldo Fieschi, an accomplished church lawyer and the son of a noble family. He took the name Innocent IV.

The emperor was polite to the new pope until Innocent demanded the emperor return some conquered papal lands. The emperor responded by stirring up angry mobs against the pope. That summer things got so dangerous that Innocent put on a disguise and secretly left Rome. He moved to France, and he was welcomed there.

Innocent IV called a meeting of bishops to condemn the emperor, but most bishops were afraid to attend. France and Spain supported Pope Innocent in his fight against the German emperor, but the rest of Europe was against the pope. Then Emperor Frederick died and the German empire began to fall apart. Innocent IV decided it was safe to move back to Rome.

The reign of Pope Innocent marked the high point of cathedral building in Europe. The great Cathedral of Chartres was completed during the Innocent's last years as pope, and it is widely considered to be the most glorious cathedral in the world.

The first cathedral had been built in 1140, and for two hundred years cathedrals were built all over Europe. A cathedral is a very large church and building one required hundreds of workers, some of them skilled designers and craftsmen, others peasant laborers who hauled the giant stone blocks into place. Some cathedrals took hundreds of years to be completed.

Figure 10 - Medieval Cathedral Towering Above a Town

The great cathedrals continue to inspire awe with their soaring vaulted ceilings and magnificent stained glass windows. They were commonly decorated with great art and often had majestic pipe organs and singers.

To impoverished peasants in the Middle Ages, cathedrals gave an overwhelming demonstration of the power and glory of the Catholic Church, and perhaps a glimpse of what going to heaven was going to feel like.

Pope Innocent IV is also remembered for allowing the Inquisition to use torture to make suspected heretics confess. The Catholic Church used the inquisition to investigate and punish those who refuse to follow the teachings of the church. Although the church in Rome determined who was a heretic, how they were punished was a decision made by the local authorities.

Once Pope Innocent let his inquisitors use torture to obtain confessions, some of them began to commit horrible atrocities. In parts of Europe the Inquisition continued to be no more than a simple investigation and interrogation, but elsewhere in Europe the Inquisition became extremely harsh.

If an accused heretic confessed, the punishment depended on the location. In northern Europe punishments were often mild, but in other places the penalty was a gruesome death. The Inquisition also made violent attacks on other groups, especially Jews and people accused of being witches.

Pope Innocent declared to everyone that he had power over all earthly kings. He even sent a representative to the Mongol Khan, leader of a huge Asian empire, saying he was in charge of all the people on earth including non-Christians. Innocent warned the Khan that the pope would have to punish the Mongols if they did not obey the Ten Commandments.

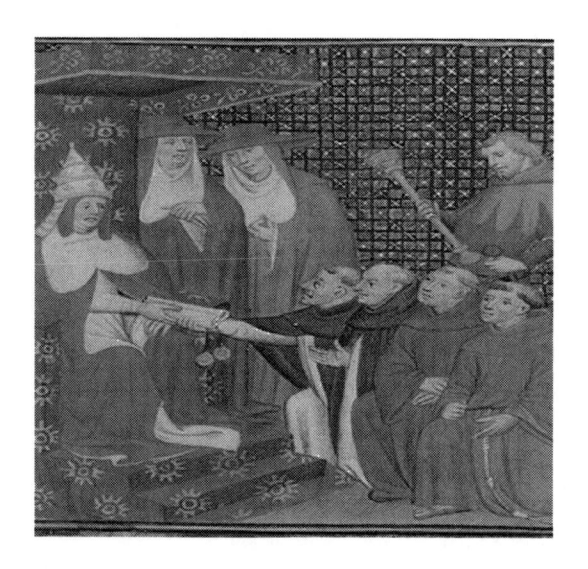

Figure 11: Pope Innocent sends a message to the Mongol Khan

The Khan sent a letter back ordering the pope and all the kings of Europe to surrender immediately to the Mongols.

The pope decided instead to capture Sicily and turn it into part of the Papal States. He needed money so he raised taxes in his kingdom until the people became restless. Pope Innocent IV was sick in bed when he learned that his army had been defeated. The bad news seemed to hasten his death, which came a few days later.

POPE BONIFACE VIII (1293-1303)

Boniface VIII came from a wealthy family and worked as a diplomat for the church He visited most of Europe before he was elected pope. Pope Celestine V had resigned as pope a few days earlier, and the first thing Pope Boniface did was have the old pope imprisoned in a castle where he soon died. Boniface VIII then enriched his family by giving them all jobs in the papal palace.

Pope Boniface began his reign by announcing the only way anyone could get into heaven was by obeying the pope's orders. His attempts to control Europe's kings and princes led to constant quarrels.

Boniface VIII could be ferocious against those who did not agree with him. For instance, the pope promised not to harm a city belonging to one of his foes if it surrendered peacefully. The city surrendered, but the pope then broke his promise and destroyed it completely, even spreading salt on the ruins so nothing would ever grow there.

The Kings of England and France announced they were going to tax the churches in their kingdoms. Boniface VIII told them "God has set popes over kings and kingdoms". The King of France responded by halting the flow of money going from churches in France to the pope in Rome. He also accused Pope Boniface of being a sodomite who abused little boys; the pope was alleged to have said that having sex with boys was 'no worse than rubbing one hand against the other'.

Boniface VIII needed money to keep fighting his many enemies. He proclaimed a Holy Year Jubilee in the year 1300, and huge crowds of pilgrims swarmed into Rome. The jubilee was a great success and brought in a lot of money. This was the first but not the last of Roman jubilees.

Pope Boniface began dressing in imperial robes like a Roman emperor. He announced that: "every creature in the world is subject to the pope."

The French King Phillip IV refused to take orders from the pope. For the first time in history he called a meeting of the three 'estates' in France: 'those that fight' (the nobles), 'those that pray' (the clergy), and 'those that work' (the peasants, who made up 90 to 95% of the population).

Each class agreed they support their king in his fight with the pope. Some of the French clergy later defied their king and attended a council meeting with Boniface in Rome. There the council declared once again that all kings must obey orders from the pope.

The French king answered this by sending a mercenary army into Italy. Boniface was kidnapped and ordered to resign. "I would sooner die!" Boniface said.

They beat him for three days and threatened to execute him. The pope was rescued, but died soon after. Some say he committed suicide by chewing on his own arm and banging his head into a wall, but this seems unlikely.

Pope Boniface's fight with French King Phillip had another result. Soon after Boniface's death the king's influence resulted in a French pope being elected. The new pope, Clement V, moved to Avignon in southern France, and for the next seventy years that became the headquarters of the Catholic Church instead of Rome.

POPE CLEMENT VI (1342-1352)

Clement VI was the fourth pope to live in Avignon, France, and these popes are famous for living in grand style. When Clement VI was first elected pope he announced his plans to live like a king, saying "my predecessors did not know how to be a pope." Clement was probably the most extravagant of them all.

He lived in the utmost luxury, holding enormous banquets and incredibly lavish parties. He was completely shameless about giving his friends and families high-paying jobs in the church. Clement spent the church's money on extravagant living, and had a reputation as a friendly and generous patron of the arts who supported many artists and musicians.

The people of Rome had elected their own antipope, but when Clement was elected they invited him to come visit Rome. Clement refused. He was afraid he would be held there and he preferred his life of luxury in Avignon; more than half of the pope's income now came from France. In 1348 the pope bought the entire city of Avignon and the surrounding countryside from the Queen of Naples.

Clement VI did try to appease the Romans by agreeing to hold a jubilee in Rome every fifty years in order to bring more tourist money into their city. He also spent a lot of money to influence politics in Italy.

In order to raise more money, Pope Clement confirmed the church policy of selling indulgences to people who wanted their sins forgiven without having to spend painful time in purgatory before going to heaven. Clement VI also began claiming he was a direct descendant of St Peter.

Pope Clement kept trying to expand his lands and influence in Europe. He ordered a new crusade to the Holy Land, but none of Europe's kings had much enthusiasm for the idea. Clement VI didn't get along well with kings. Pope Clement argued with the Holy Roman Emperor and ex-communicated him. He also had disputes with the King of England, the King of Poland, the King of Hungary, and two Spanish kings.

Then the Black Death swept through Europe. It continued for three years and almost half the people in Europe were killed by this great pandemic. It took 150 years to restore the population of Europe.

An Italian shoemaker named Agnola kept a diary during this terrible plague. He said: "They died by the hundreds, both day and night, and all were thrown in ditches and covered with dirt. And as soon as those ditches were filled, more were dug. And I, Agnola di Tura buried my five children with my own hands... And so many died that all believed it was the end of the world."

It was a common belief that the plague was God's way of punishing people for their sins. Many people became flagellants who whipped and beat themselves, believing they needed to punish themselves for the sins of their flesh. They often wandered from town to town in long processions, beating themselves every few steps.

Most wealthy people fled from the disease-ridden cities to live in the countryside until the plague died out. But Pope Clement remained in Avignon where he visited the sick and attended funerals. He granted forgiveness of all sins to those who died of the Black Death. Pope Clement VI never caught the disease.

As he lay dying in 1352 he said: "I have lived as a sinner among sinners."

Figure 12- 'The Black Death'

POPE URBAN VI (1378-1389)

When Pope Gregory XI died, an angry Roman mob gathered to make sure the cardinals did not choose a pope who would move back to France. The cardinals compromised on a man who was not connected to any of the wealthy families. Pope Urban VI had been a simple and devout French monk, but he surprised the cardinals. Instead of being easy to control, he turned out to be an arrogant, violent, and very unstable man.

Urban VI began his reign by promising he would stay in Rome and not move the papacy back to France. The French King was not pleased. Then Urban forbid the cardinals to accept gifts or payments, and he condemned their lives of luxury and their many servants.

The cardinals thought the new pope had gone insane. The French cardinals invited the pope to meet with them in France. Urban feared he would be killed or imprisoned so he refused.

The cardinals then declared that the election had been illegal because the angry Roman mobs had forced them to elect an Italian. They elected a French anti-pope, Clement VII. The antipope declared that Pope Urban was "the anti-Christ", and war broke out.

The war in northern Italy involved extreme cruelty. Urban proved to be unstable, unreasonable and unable to make good decisions. He offended his allies and was betrayed by those he trusted. When Rome itself was invaded, Pope Urban escaped to join his ally in southern Italy.

When he arrived, the man he thought was a faithful ally seized the pope and locked him up. Pope Urban managed to escape to northern Italy. Several of his faithful cardinals followed him, hoping they could convince the pope that his situation was hopeless and he had to make peace.

Instead, when the cardinals made their suggestion, Urban had them all arrested, gruesomely tortured, and then executed five of them.

This act shocked his remaining supporters. The pope's finances and administrative offices were collapsing around him. Urban VI managed to assemble an army of mercenaries, raising the money he needed by announcing another jubilee would be held in Rome in 1390.

But Pope Urban fell off his mule while with his army, and he went back to Rome to recover. He died there soon after, perhaps from his fall, although poisoning seems more likely.

POPE BONIFACE IX (1389-1404)

There was already another pope in France, the anti-pope Clement VI, when Boniface IX was elected as pope in Rome.

Catholics in Europe were divided into two camps: Pope Boniface had support from most of Italy and from England, Germany, Hungary and Poland. The rest of Europe recognized Clement VI as the true pope. The two popes quickly ex-communicated each other.

When the church split in two, Boniface IX only received half the income of former popes. But he had a plenty of expenses.

Like most popes, he spent a lot of church money on his friends and family. He paid to fortify his headquarters in Rome and to keep the threatening mobs there under control; he often left Rome and lived in the countryside just to be safe.

Pope Boniface also needed a steady supply of cash to pay the soldiers in his large army. His army was able to defeat the forces of anti-pope Clement, but Boniface IX still needed an army to keep the French king from invading Italy. The pope also planned to recapture the lost cities and castles in his money-making Papal States.

Boniface tried everything he could think of to raise money. He held two jubilees to attract visitors to Rome. The first was fairly successful and encouraged him to organize a bigger one ten years later, which drew pilgrims from all over Europe including many from France.

The pope also raised money by selling dispensations (which forgave sins) and indulgences (which allowed the recently dead to go straight to heaven without having to wait in painful purgatory). This did cause some scandal.

The sale of benefices in England became even more scandalous. A benefice can be any source of payments or small salaries that came to a church. The pope's agents would sell vacant benefices to the highest bidder, usually one of Boniface's Roman friends.

They also sold the future rights to benefices before they were vacant, and in the meantime if a higher bidder came along then Pope Boniface would cancel the first sale. One observer said he saw the same benefice sold several times in one week, and that even during mass the pope talked about business with his secretaries.

The Kings of Europe began pushing Boniface to abdicate, leaving just one pope in charge of the continent. Pope Boniface refused to quit. While he was pope, no councils were held to discuss unifying the church. Instead, Boniface IX tried to organize a new crusade against the

Muslims; the kings were not enthusiastic and nothing happened.

In 1404 Pope Boniface met with representatives of the new French antipope Benedict XIII. It turned into an angry shouting match, and Pope Boniface died two days later. His staff blamed the antipope's men and threw them in prison. They were only released after the French paid a huge ransom to the Roman church.

In an age when so many kings and popes were greedy and corrupt, many people still believe Pope Boniface IX was the most corrupt of them all.

POPE PAUL II (1464-1471)

Paul was a nephew of Pope Eugenius IV so he advanced rapidly when he joined the church. He was a generous man, and promised that if they elected him pope he would buy each of the cardinals a house in the countryside. It was no surprise when the cardinals' votes were counted and Paul became the new pope.

One cardinal reported that Paul had wanted to take the name Formosus, which meant 'handsome', but was talked out of it. The first Formosus had been exhumed from his grave, and then his corpse was put on trial, found guilty, mutilated and thrown in the river. Paul decided to become Pope Paul II instead of Pope Handsome.

His highest priority was to have a new luxury palace built .He then filled it with art treasures. He had a papal tiara designed, made of "diamonds, sapphires, emeralds, topaz, large pearls, and every kind of precious gem."

Paul II knew how important it was to keep the restless Roman crowds entertained, so he staged popular events in Rome such as annual horse races down the main street.

The pope who came before Paul had joked that Paul should be given the nickname 'Our Lady of Pity', because Paul liked to dress up as a woman . Pope Paul had a habit of crying in order to get his way. Paul loved to dress up in elaborate costumes and to wear rouge and make-up in public.

Pope Paul II is one source of the legend of the female Pope Joan; people who saw him would tell others they had seen a woman acting as the pope.

Paul promised when he was elected to name only one of his relatives as a new cardinal, but now he nominated three of them, as well as his old teacher. Then he began to eliminate what he thought were useless jobs in Rome, many of which had been filled with friends of the other cardinals.

These cardinals became upset. One wrote a complaining letter and the pope had him imprisoned and tortured, along with other former job-holders the pope believed were conspiring against him.

Paul II died suddenly at the age of 54. His supporters said his death was caused by eating too much. His enemies said he died of a heart attack while being sodomized by a servant boy. After his death, the new pope and cardinals inspected Paul's vault and found it stacked high with gold and beautiful jewels.

The Vatican librarian who worked for Paul wrote an extremely unflattering biography, which may be part of the reason Pope Paul II is remembered as one of history's least popular popes.

Figure 13 - 'Pope Handsome'

POPE SIXTUS IV (1471-1484)

Sixtus IV became pope after the sudden and rather mysterious death of Paul II. Pope Sixtus was a very different man. He was one of the very few popes who came from a poor family. He liked to read and had been a university lecturer, but he didn't know much about the business side of the church. Pope Sixtus gave important jobs to his family, and they began to manage things for him.

Sixtus IV ordered a new crusade against the Muslims. Money was raised, but the kings of Europe were indifferent and the crusaders didn't do much. Then the pope got involved in a power struggle in the wealthy town of Florence.

The pope's relatives in the city-state of Florence were becoming very rich, and one of them made plans to assassinate the ruling Medici brothers and put a nephew of Pope Sixtus in charge. Pope Sixtus knew about the plot but allowed it to continue.

The Medici brothers were suddenly attacked and stabbed while attending church, but one of them survived. The killers were arrested, but Pope Sixtus personally granted forgiveness to the murderers.

The surviving Medici brother ignored the pope's command and had some of the criminals hung. Pope Sixtus then declared war on Florence.

The pope also tried to capture the city of Ferrara so he could give it to another one of nephews. War spread across northern Italy, and eventually the angry Italian princes forced the unwilling Sixtus to make peace.

Sixtus knew the importance of keeping the Roman mobs under control. He restored the old Roman aqueduct so people didn't have to drink out of the polluted river anymore. He built bridges, widened roads, and repaired churches, as well as building the Sistine Chapel.

Pope Sixtus warned Portugal and Spain against taking slaves from Africa to their new colonies in South America. Sixtus told them the church had no problem with kidnapping and enslaving Africans who were not Christians, but the Africans should first be given a chance to convert to the Catholic faith.

The slave traders got around this rule by reading the offer to convert in their own languages, which the Africans didn't understand.

Sixtus also agreed to let King Ferdinand and Queen Isabella of Spain carry out an Inquisition to find and punish those who disobeyed the church. The Spanish Inquisition soon went out of control.

Sixtus also appointed many relatives and friends as new cardinals so his policies would be continued even after his death.

Figure 14 – The Inquisition Killing a Heretic

POPE INNOCENT VIII (1484-1492)

When Pope Sixtus died, the cardinals could not agree on any of the candidates for pope being pushed by the different Roman families. Rival gangs fought each other in the streets of Rome. Finally the most powerful cardinal agreed to support someone from outside his own family – someone he believed would be easy for him to control.

Bribes were paid, and that is how Giovanni Cybo became Pope Innocent VIII. He was a cardinal-priest from southern Italy who had already fathered three illegitimate children before becoming he became an ordained priest.

Soon after his election, Pope Innocent received a letter from Germany complaining about the growing number of witches there. Devil worship there was being blamed for everything from sickness and death to bad weather and poor crops.

The late Middle Ages had seen a series of catastrophes including great famines and plagues. The Little Ice Age had begun and this period of global cooling reduced the size of crops and made life harder for livestock. There was hunger and social unrest all over Europe.

Figure 15 - Devil Worshippers

Belief in both good and bad magic was common among the peasants, and many blamed Satan and his helpers for their troubles. The church had always rejected any belief in witches, but during the Middle Ages this church policy changed.

In 1484 Pope Innocent VIII recognized the existence of witches and gave full approval for the Inquisition to do whatever was necessary to get rid of them.

There was widespread hysteria, and witch-hunts went on for over two hundred years, even reaching North America.

Most of the accused witches were women, and large numbers of these women were burned alive in Germany and France. All women accused of being witches were stripped naked and searched inside and out by their inquisitors. One famous victim was Joan of Arc, accused by a bishop of witchcraft, and of "dressing like a male". Joan was tortured for four days, and then burned at the stake.

Trials required evidence to convict an accused witch. All that was necessary was for someone to accuse someone of being a witch and the prosecutors would try to get a confession. They often used extreme violence such as red-hot pincers, the thumbscrew, or holding the suspect underwater for long periods. If someone confessed then the penalty was usually death, for the bible said "Thou shalt not suffer a witch to live."

Pope Innocent called for a new crusade against the Muslims when he was first elected pope, but few people were enthusiastic. The Muslim empire had taken over what had once been the wealthy Eastern Roman Empire based in Constantinople. The Muslims established the Ottoman Empire in its place.

The Muslims had been invaded Europe but had been pushed out of Italy, although they still held part of Spain.

Then the brother of the Ottoman Sultan suddenly arrived in the west, asking for help from the pope to overthrow the Sultan. The pope considered this, but instead locked the rebellious brother in prison. The Ottoman Sultan agreed to give the pope a large payment every year to keep the treacherous brother locked up far away from Constantinople.

Innocent VIII kept expanding and renovating his palaces and castles, and he always needed more money. He invented new church titles and auctioned them off to the highest bidders. He also charged kings a fee for taking part in their coronation ceremonies. When the King of Naples refused to pay, Innocent ex-communicated him and invited the King of France to invade. Pope Innocent VIII died in 1492, the same year the Spanish captured Granada and drove the Muslims entirely out of Europe.

The pope left behind two illegitimate children. Pope Innocent had made them both very rich during his reign as pope. Innocent's oldest son married a Medici and was the father of Pope Leo X. It is said that when Pope Innocent VIII was dying, he begged the cardinals to pick a better man as the next pope.

POPE ALEXANDER VI (1492-1503)

Alexander VI was a member of the infamous Spanish Borgia family, and a relative of most of Europe's kings and queens. He had a series of mistresses and fathered several illegitimate children while he was a cardinal in Rome. Alexander was already rich and had years of experience in administering the church by the time he was elected pope.

There were rumors that he had paid bribes to win the election. It is certainly true that the three leading candidates for the job spent a lot of money trying to become pope. The new pope started by treating everyone fairly and he encouraged good church government, although he did make sure all his relatives did well at the church's expense. He appointed twelve new cardinals including his young son and the brother of one of his mistresses.

One of his favorite mistresses bore him four children that he openly admitted were his own. He is known to have had at least seven other illegitimate children. Pope Alexander became the ancestor of almost all the royal families of Europe in the years to come. He loved his children and loaded them with honors and wealth while he was pope.

Pope Alexander was soon involved in the many fights and feuds going on between Europe's different kings. Spain agreed to support Alexander VI, perhaps because Alexander had was about to draw a line dividing newly discovered South America between Spain and Portugal. The line Pope Alexander chose gave Brazil to Portugal and everything else to the king of Spain.

French armies invaded southern Italy and the papal lands were in danger. Soon the King of France was marching his army close to Rome. Pope Alexander desperately tried to organize a defense; he even asked the Ottoman Sultan for help, but to no avail. As the French marched into Rome, Alexander was afraid their king would name a new pope.

Alexander VI promised the king's favorite bishop a promotion to cardinal if he would help arrange peace terms. King Charles VIII of France did agree to a peace treaty in exchange for one of the pope's cities and a valuable hostage (the Sultan's imprisoned brother). The French army then marched south and captured the Kingdom of Naples instead.

The rest of Europe's kings were frightened by the growing power of France, and they joined forces with the pope to form "the Holy League". They pretended their purpose was to fight the Muslims, but instead their armies pushed the French out of Italy. Alexander VI tried to take advantage of the weakened state of his neighbors to expand his own kingdom, the Papal States, but his army was not strong enough.

Tragedy struck the pope when his son Giovanni was found murdered. His body was discovered floating in the river, gold coins still in his pocket. The servant who had been with him was also killed. There were no witnesses, but rumors spread that he had been killed by one of his own brothers.

Pope Alexander was overcome by grief and promised to dedicate the rest of his life to reforming the church. However he soon returned to the sexuality and corruption that were making his reign infamous. There were rumors that his family, the Borgia, used murder and blackmail to raise money to pay for their extravagant lifestyle. These accusations have never been completely proven.

Figure 16 - Pope Alexander VI, his favorite mistress as the Virgin Mary, and their infant son as baby Jesus

The behavior of the pope and those around him became so scandalous that a friar named Savonarola appealed for a council to confront papal abuses and corruption. It is said Pope Alexander laughed when he read the accusations against him. There was chaos in Florence where many people supported Savonarola's fiery condemnation of Pope Alexander. By 1498 Savonarola had clearly gone too far, and the pope had him burned alive.

Rich families in Italy began to unite against Alexander VI, and the pope decided the only people he could truly trust were his family. He arranged marriages for his relatives with noble families all over Europe to gain allies and lands. With the French as an ally, the pope was strong enough to attack his enemies in Italy, killing or imprisoning many of them.

Then one evening after a dinner with one of his cardinals, the pope and his son Cesare suddenly became very ill. Pope Alexander VI died a few days later. Cesare ordered his servants to seize the pope's treasure before the death was publicly announced.

The next day the pope's body was shown to the public; apparently the body was decomposing very rapidly and the tongue "was inflated by poison." Custom required worshippers to kiss the body, but nobody dared.

POPE JULIUS II (1503-1513)

Julius II was elected pope soon after the very sudden death by poison of Pope Alexander VI. Julius came from a wealthy family, and was promoted to cardinal at a very young age while his uncle Sixtus was pope. Julius spent several years as the pope's representative in France, fathering an illegitimate daughter while he was there.

Julius was one of the rich but unsuccessful candidates for pope in the papal election won by Pope Alexander VI. Fearing revenge, Julius moved to Paris after his defeat and urged the French King to invade Italy. When Alexander died, the cardinals elected Pius III to replace him. But Pius himself died suddenly just a few weeks later, perhaps from an ulcer, perhaps by being poisoned.

Now Julius made a deal with Cesare Borgia, Pope Alexander's son, to gain his support in the new election. Cesare was still very ill after being poisoned at the same time as his father Pope Alexander VI. He agreed to use his power to help get Julius elected in exchange for a promise from Julius to support the Borgia family. Many bribes were paid and almost all the cardinals voted for Julius.

When Julius II became pope he ignored the promises he had made. He used his power to weaken the Borgia family, and he refused to live in the same rooms used by the Borgia pope Alexander.

He said: "Alexander VI desecrated the holy church like no one before, he usurped the papal power by the devil's aid... his name and memory must be forgotten." He ordered the Borgia's tombs to be opened and their bodies sent back to their homelands in Spain. The rooms they had lived in remained sealed for centuries.

The new pope also ordered the destruction of the ancient basilica in Rome, and commissioned the enormous St Peter's Basilica to be built in its place. In the very center of the magnificent new basilica he ordered a gigantic tomb for himself, several stories high and decorated with carvings and sculptures by artists like Michelangelo.

Pope Julius was a true patron of the arts, and commissioned dozens of paintings and sculptures from Raphael and Michelangelo. It was Julius who forced Michelangelo to paint the ceiling of the Sistine Chapel.

Figure 17 – Picture of God's face from Sistine Chapel Ceiling by Michelangelo

Julius II also loved war, and fought a series of battles which earned him the nickname "The Fearsome Pope". He loved to strap on his armor and personally lead his soldiers into battle.

His armies captured cities and castles across northern Italy. He took pride in presenting himself as the leader of an empire; he considered himself to be a modern-day Julius Caesar.

But after his French allies defeated Venice, they refused to leave the pope in charge of Italy. The pope attacked his former allies, and with help from the German Emperor he drove the French out of Italy. However his new allies also refused to leave northern Italy. Julius controlled the area around Rome, but he died before he could fulfill his dream of ruling a united Italy.

POPE LEO X (1513-1521)

After Pope Julius II died, the cardinals elected as new pope the second son of Lorenzo the Magnificent, head of the Medici family. He was the last non-priest to be elected Pope. After being elected on March 9, he was ordained a priest on March 15, consecrated as bishop on March 17, and crowned Pope Leo X two days later.

It was the height of the Renaissance in Italy, and it is said when he became pope Leo told his brother: "Since God has given us the papacy, let us enjoy it." He enjoyed riding in parades around Rome mounted on his white elephant named Hanno. Pope Leo spent money on Roman hospitals, on the Roman University, and he gave generously to the poor.

Leo X was a cultured man and loved music, books, and great art. He spent a fortune rebuilding St Peter's Basilica on a huge scale, and hired Raphael to decorate the Vatican. He also loved enormous parties and feasts; some of his meals had more than sixty courses. Pope Leo needed a lot of money, and he borrowed heavily.

Most of the money was spent on warfare. Leo X was immediately drawn into the wars in northern Italy. He joined with Spain and Germany to prevent the French from taking over, but after losing a battle in 1515 the pope made a separate and secret peace agreement with the French. The fighting stopped for a while and a general peace seemed possible.

Then England gave Pope Leo enough money to raise a new army and soon war raged again. It cost a fortune, but in the end Leo X was able to create a new state around the city of Urbino, and he made his younger brother the duke.

The war left the church bankrupt, and several cardinals plotted to poison Leo. The pope's spies discovered the plot in time: Leo had their leader executed and put the others in prison. He then appointed 31 new cardinals who owed their loyalty to him. Some of them paid the pope handsomely for the privilege.

Then the pope decided to launch a new crusade against the Turks, who were threatening to invade Europe. This project was going to cost a lot of money, and Leo X had already spent all the money Julius II had saved. Pope Leo increased the share of income and crops that believers had to give to the church. He also pushed his representatives to sell more indulgences to raise money. He borrowed money from bankers and rich families, and he even sold palace furniture and jewels.

Despite all these efforts to raise money, the rest of Leo's reign as pope was spent in a state of financial crisis. Even worse for the

Catholic Church, the methods Leo X was using to raise money were causing people to get angry and restless all over Europe. Pope Leo had sent his 'papal commissioners' across Europe to sell indulgences, and in October 1517 a German clergyman named Martin Luther had started a protest that quickly gained the support of thousands of German Catholics.

The Catholic Church taught that when someone died, they could not go to heaven until they were punished for all their sins on earth. Their soul had to burn in purgatory for a period that might last centuries depending on their sins. St Augustine, an African bishop writing a thousand years earlier, taught that these fires were "more painful than anything a man can suffer in this life".

Pope Leo's representatives promised to cancel purgatory and send the dead person's soul directly to heaven in exchange for a payment. They used a hard sell, telling the poor and uneducated people to pay up, otherwise their dead children and parents would have to spend centuries burning in the agonizing flames of purgatory.

Martin Luther objected to the threats used to sell these 'tickets to heaven', and the sales jingle they used: "As soon as the coin in the coffer rings, the soul from purgatory springs". He asked: "Why does the pope, whose wealth today is greater than Crassus, build the basilica of St Peter with the money of poor believers instead of his own money?"

Church doors were often used as community bulletin boards, so Luther nailed his list of complaints to the door of his church. He demanded that the church reform itself. The printing press was a recent invention that made books much smaller and cheaper, allowing Luther's complaints to circulate widely. Luther translated the bible from Latin into German so everyone could read it; the Gutenberg Bible helped the Protestant Reformation spread rapidly across northern Europe.

Leo X responded by ex-communicating Luther and urging the kings of Europe to persecute anyone who denied the teachings of the Catholic Church. Instead, some northern countries began to expel the pope's representatives. Many of the local clergy were also unhappy with the orders they were receiving from Rome. Leo wanted to stamp out these rebellions, but his armies were still fighting in Italy.

In November 1521 Pope Leo X rejoiced at the news that his armies had captured the province of Milan. Then he died unexpectedly, probably from pneumonia. Several banks and many individuals were ruined when Pope Leo died so suddenly still owing them enormous sums of money.

POPE CLEMENT VII (1523-1534)

Pope Clement VII was another Medici pope and a cousin of Leo X. When he became pope he immediately became involved in the war waging inside Italy.

The French had captured the rich city-state of Milan, so the pope abandoned his German and Spanish allies and made peace with France. When the French king was beaten in battle and captured, the pope switched sides and signed a new alliance with his old partners. Then the French King was set free, and the pope switched sides for a third time.

The German emperor called the pope 'a wolf instead of a shepherd'. Several powerful families in Rome turned against Pope Clement and supported the emperor. The soldiers of the Colonna family took control of Rome and looted the Vatican. Pope Clement had no choice; to save himself he switched his allegiance again and rejoined the German emperor's side. But when Cardinal Colonna led his army off to fight in Naples, the Pope quickly announced he was once again supporting the King of French.

The German emperor's forces overwhelmed Italy and reached Rome. The leader of this army was killed during a short siege, and his hungry and unpaid soldiers went out of control. They looted the city for days, raping and murdering the unfortunate people who remained there.

Pope Clement himself fled to one of his castles in the countryside. He was captured by the Germans and forced to pay a huge ransom. The pope also had to give up many of the Italian cities he owned. The Republic of Venice took advantage of this situation by using their own army to capture several more of his cities.

The pope returned to Rome in 1528, finding most of the city in complete ruins and very few people still living there.

Clement VII had other problems during this time of troubles. English King Henry VIII wanted a divorce from his wife Catherine because she could not have children. She was the aunt of the German emperor, whose troops had just destroyed Rome. Pope Clement was afraid to grant the divorce in case he made the emperor angry.

King Henry had the Archbishop of Canterbury annul the marriage. He then married Anne Boleyn and they had a daughter who became Queen Elizabeth I. The pope ex-communicated both the King and the archbishop. Henry VIII passed a law that allowed him to keep all the money that English churches used to send to the Pope. Henry VIII declared that the Kingdom of England was leaving the Catholic Church, and he established the Church of England, independent of Rome's control.

The European powers finally made peace with each other. Some of the lost lands were restored to the pope, including the wealthy city-state of Florence. Pope Clement appointed his illegitimate son as the Duke of Florence.

For the rest of his life Pope Clement obeyed the German emperor, although he kept trying to convince the emperor to crack down hard on the Lutheran Protestants in Germany. Clement began thinking about switching sides again by joining a French alliance, but in September 1534 he died. The official cause of death was a poison mushroom.

A famous miracle was reported during the reign of Pope Clement VII. A vision of the Virgin Mary mysteriously appeared near Guadalupe, Mexico in 1531 in front of an Aztec man named Juan Diego. The Virgin told Juan that his gravely ill uncle would get better if Juan took some roses to the bishop. When Juan reached the bishop's house he unfolded his cloak and the flowers spilled out, leaving a clear impression of the Virgin Mary on his cloak.

The uncle did get better, and the bishop declared it was a miracle. He had a shrine built on the spot where the Virgin Mary had appeared. The original cloak is still on display in Guadalupe, the shrine is one of the world's busiest pilgrimage sites. New Virgin sightings were soon reported elsewhere, including Bolivia, Cuba, Argentina and Costa Rica.

Figure 18 - Our Lady of Guadalupe

Juan's story about 'Our Lady of Guadalupe' led to rapid growth of the Catholic faith all over Mexico. In the seven years that followed the Virgin of Guadalupe's appearance, an estimated eight million native people joined the Catholic Church. Over the coming years, the Catholic Church became one of biggest landholders in Latin America. Juan was made a saint.

POPE PAUL III (1534-1549)

Pope Paul III was a member of the wealthy Farnese family. His family became much richer after Paul became pope.

He was a promiscuous pope who kept a mistress while he was pope. He had already fathered four illegitimate children with a noble Roman mistress. His own sister Giulia had been the mistress of Pope Alexander VI.

The first thing Pope Paul did was to appoint his grandsons as cardinals. Some of them were very young to become cardinals: Alessandro was 14 years old, Ranuccio was 15, and Guido was 16. Paul III then appointed a long line of his nephews as cardinals.

Paul's favorite project was using church money to build a magnificent family palace in central Rome, the Palazzo Farnese. He filled it with the most beautiful and expensive works of art he could find. He also built the Villa Farnese in the countryside. He hired Michelangelo to paint frescoes for him, and Titian to paint portraits of the new pope and his family.

Pope Paul knew how to keep the often unruly Romans happy. He revived the Carnival and delighted Romans with bullfights and horse races. He also built new defensive fortifications in Rome and the Papal States.

Paul III had a tricky relationship with the German emperor. The emperor was pushing the pope to resolve his differences with the Protestant followers of Martin Luther in Germany. Paul was reluctant to open the door to reform of the church, but he did choose nine high-ranking clergy to report on how the church should be reformed.

Their report exposed "gross abuses" in the church and suggested several bold ways of abolishing those abuses. Martin Luther and his Protestants complained that the report did not go far enough. The pope was eager to show the emperor that he was willing to reform, but in fact nothing was done and the recommendations for change were ignored in Rome.

The pope was busy with other matters. Paul III wanted to make one of his grandsons a duke, but to accomplish that would require him to seize a city by force. But by now his expenses had grown so large he had to raise taxes in the states he controlled. Soon his subjects were on the verge of revolt. One city-state owned by the Colonna family actually did revolt, and was besieged by an army led by one of Pope Paul's sons. The son was successful, and the rebels were defeated.

Pope Paul decided to control his subjects using the Congregation of the Holy Office of the Inquisition. They began searching out and suppressing heretics in Italy. The Inquisition eventually got a bad name, so the name was changed to The Sacred Congregation of the Holy Office in 1908, then renamed again as The Congregation for the Doctrine of the Faith in 1965.

The Vatican made rules for what kind of torture could be used by the Inquisition. Clergy who wanted to work for the Inquisition were even given special training by the church's torture experts. The most popular ways to get a confession included roasting the suspect's feet over a fire or stretching them on a rack until their body began to rip apart. Many victims confessed immediately simply to avoid the torture.

Once an accused heretic confessed, they were tied to a stake and burned to death in a public spectacle. There were many abuses, and the inquisition became very unpopular.

Figure 19 – The Inquisition at Work

Some inquisitors would condemn a heretic just so they could confiscate his property for themselves. They also sold absolutions for a price, allowing heretics to buy forgiveness.

Pope Paul officially recognized a new society dedicated to defending the faith. These became known as the Jesuits, sometimes called 'God's Soldiers'. The pope set in motion a deliberate campaign against the Protestants.

The German emperor had told the pope find a peaceful way to make peace with the protesters, but now he changed his mind. The emperor was using force to subdue rebellious protestant princes in his empire, and he wanted the pope to help.

The pope agreed to send troops and money to help the emperor, but in exchange he wanted to be given lands that he could use to make his son Pier Luigi a duke. The emperor agreed. Open warfare began in Germany, and the emperor quickly re-established his power over all his territories. This restored Germany to the Catholic Church. But the pope was not happy.

The emperor had agreed to permit the pope's son to become a duke. But when the son tried to act as duke, one of the emperor's strongest supporters used force to throw the pope's son out of town.

A short while later, the pope's son was assassinated. The pope believed this could not have happened without the emperor knowing about it in advance.

Pope Paul demanded that he be given his son's inheritance in the name of the church, but the rightful heir refused to give it up and was supported by the emperor. That heir was Cardinal Ottavio Farnese, a grandson of the pope.

There was a violent altercation between the pope and his grandson. Pope Paul III was 81 years old, and it was said the shock of that confrontation led to his feverish death a few days later.

POPE JULIUS III (1550-1555)

After Paul III died, three groups of cardinals met to choose a new pope in 1549. One group supported the German emperor, one group supported the French King, and the third group supported the Farnese family. They finally agreed on a cardinal who did not come from any of these factions, and Giovanni del Monte became Pope Julius III.

The new pope wanted to reform the Catholic Church, but despite the talk there was very little action. The German emperor pushed Julius into entering a league against France. The pope quickly made peace with the French. He occasionally set up a commission to study reform of the church but he made no strong effort to accomplish any actual reforms.

Pope Julius was content to relax in the luxury of a palace he had built for himself in Rome. At first, the worst thing people had to say about the new pope was that he ate onions by the cartload. Then a scandal began to grow around the pope's relationship with a teenage boy.

The pope's family had hired a young beggar boy named Innocenzo to work in their family home as a servant. After Julius became pope, he convinced his brother to adopt the boy into the del Monte family.

Pope Julius appears to have fallen in love with the boy. He appointed him as a cardinal and gave him plenty of church benefices (payments made to the church from various sources). Rumours began to circulate about the pope's unusual relationship with the boy.

People began to make fun of Julius, although many others were seriously shocked by his behavior. They wondered why the pope had appointed the boy who took care of his monkey as a new cardinal. The ambassador from Venice reported that Innocenzo slept in the same bed as Julius.

The pope's supporters suggested that perhaps the boy was just an illegitimate son. That might explain their loving relationship and all the favors Julius lavished on him. The pope began to spend most of his time at a luxury villa he had built with church money.

The scandal began to make the church a laughing-stock. When Pope Julius died, the church tried to leave the scandal behind. However Innocenzo was involved in the murder of two men who insulted him, and he was banished for a while. He returned to Rome, but after the rape of two women he was banished again. He was sent to prison and later died in obscurity, the same way he had started out in life.

Figure 20 - Pope Julius III loved his Monkey-Boy

POPE PAUL IV (1555-1559)

Paul IV was a surprise choice for pope. He was already 79 years old, and he had a reputation for being a cranky and difficult man.

His main accomplishment had been as a cardinal when he organized a Roman Inquisition modeled on the Spanish Inquisition. He was one of the Inquisitors himself, and once said: "Even if my own father were a heretic, I would gather the wood to burn him."

One of Pope Paul's first actions was to hire an artist to paint underwear on the nude figures Michelangelo had painted on the ceiling of the Sistine Chapel. This artist became known around Rome as 'the panty-painter'. The pope also cut elderly Michelangelo's pension.

Pope Paul introduced an Index of Prohibited Books, listing all the books he did not want Catholics to read. The Index banned a lot of books, including all books written by Protestants.

It also prohibited Catholics from reading any bibles printed in languages the common people could understand, such as Italian or German. Pope Paul feared that Catholics might lose their faith in him if they were free to study modern ideas and discoveries. He imprisoned the cardinals who disagreed with him.

Pope Paul IV was particularly harsh toward Jews. He said God had condemned the Jews to eternal servitude and they deserved to be kept in slavery. He forced Jews to wear distinctive yellow hats, and at night the gates of their walled ghettos were locked shut.

The pope drove England even further away from the Catholic Church. Paul told Queen Elizabeth I that she would have to let him approve all her claims, and that she must pay him for church property confiscated by the Protestants.

Although Paul IV was cruel to those he disliked, he took good care of his family. He gave them high-ranking jobs in the church and helped them prosper in their careers. His nephew Carlo became his chief advisor and they made plans to join forces with France in an attack against Spain, even though it was the most Catholic country in Europe.

The war with Spain was an expensive disaster. Everyone in Rome said the pope was the only man who did not know the two nephews he trusted the most were really thieves and scoundrels.

After several scandals the pope realized the truth and exiled them. It was said this broke the old man's heart - Pope Paul IV died at the age of 83.

Nobody mourned his death. The Roman Inquisition had been too harsh and after his death the Roman people rioted and destroyed the Inquisition's headquarters in Rome. They also decapitated the pope's statue. The next pope had Paul's nephews put to death.

POPE PIUS V (1566-1572)

When Antonio Ghislieri became Pope Pius V it was quite a move up in the world for a poor shepherd boy from northern Italy. He had always been very religious, and at age fourteen had became a monk. He became an inquisitor, angry at how immoral the some people in the church had become. The cardinals who chose him wanted a pope who would prevent Catholics from becoming rebellious.

Pope Pius immediately went to work to restore morality inside the Vatican. He tightened up expenses and reduced spending as much as he could. The new pope put an end to all the lavish feasts and made everyone in the Vatican live a strict lifestyle.

He also began to 'clean up' Rome by expelling beggars and prostitutes. He insisted that canon law (the laws of the church) be firmly enforced, and he made a common mass standard throughout the church.

The new pope took a very dim view of Protestants and led attacks against them, particularly against the Huguenots in France. The violence reached its peak with the St Bartholomew's Day Massacre. Catholics murdered as many as 25,000 Protestants in

Paris alone, followed by similar massacres in other French towns. An amnesty was then granted and the Pope Pius pardoned all the killers.

Pope Pius V also supported a Catholic uprising in England. He declared Queen Elizabeth deposed and ex-communicated. He released all her subjects from any oaths of allegiance they had made to her.

The queen was not amused. She had been quite tolerant of English Catholics who worshipped in private, but now she began persecuting them for treason.

The pope's greatest accomplishment was forming the Holy League to fight off a Turkish invasion of Europe. The Turkish Muslims had captured Cyprus after promising to let the Christian soldiers leave if they stopped fighting, Then the Muslims broke their promise and imprisoned them all, flaying and beheading their commanders.

Pius V organized the Catholic nations around the Mediterranean Sea to fight the Turkish fleet. The two huge fleets fought it out at the Battle of Lepanto in 1571. The Turks had more ships, but the European ships had more guns. At the end of the day the Turks were totally destroyed.

The Holy League's admirals gave credit for their victory to help they received from the Virgin Mary. It was said that Pope Pius had a vision of the victory on the day of the battle. He died a year later.

Years later the church decided it was a miracle that Pope Pius knew the battle was won even though he was in Rome at the time. Pope Pius V was canonized as a saint.

POPE URBAN VIII (1623-1644)

Maffeo Barberini came from a rich Italian family and took the name Urban VIII when he became pope. He immediately began using his powers as pope to make his family even richer. Their expenses became a huge drain on the church treasury, but his immediate family became millionaires.

Urban himself loved elegant living and spent church money to hire artists like Bernini and Poussin to decorate buildings in Rome.

Pope Urban was an educated man who wrote poetry and enjoyed the company of great thinkers. He spent a lot of money bringing them to Rome so he could speak with them. One of these men was Galileo, one of the greatest scientists to ever live. Urban VIII and Galileo became friends, and Urban encouraged his scientific work.

This friendship ended abruptly when Galileo announced that Copernicus had been correct and the earth was not at the center of the universe. This contradicted what the church had been teaching for centuries, so Pope Urban condemned Copernicus (who was already dead) and sent the Inquisition to interrogate Galileo.

At his final interrogation Galileo was threatened with torture if he did not tell the truth. He maintained his denial despite the threat, but then he was threatened with execution.

To avoid being tortured and killed, Galileo confessed that he had made a mistake. Pope Urban then sentenced him to life in prison. Because Galileo was now in his old age, Urban let Galileo serve this sentence at home.

The reign of Pope Urban VIII coincided with most of the Thirty-Years War, fought between the Catholic and Protestant nations of Europe. This war was not only one of the longest wars in history, it was also one of most deadly and destructive. Most of the fighting took place in Germany and Holland; in parts of Germany three-quarters of the population were killed.

Thousands of towns and villages were completely destroyed by greedy armies of mercenary soldiers. It took the devastated German states almost a hundred years to recover.

When the war ended with the Peace of Westphalia, it was agreed that the citizens of all nations would be commanded only by their kings, not by religious authorities like the pope.

The Thirty-Years War also marked the peak of the Catholic Church's witch-hunting frenzy. As the warring armies marched back and forth across Europe they spread diseases and destroyed crops, causing famine and starvation. People often blamed the devil for their suffering.

Figure 21 – Torturing Suspected Witch

They accused their fellow citizens of being witches and engaging in devil worship. The number of witch trials and executions soared during the war. It is a tragic truth that even today women in Africa and the Middle East are being condemned to torture and death for being witches.

Pope Urban spent enormous sums of money building forts to protect his own Papal States. He fortified Rome and set up a special factory there for making cannons and other weapons. He created an arsenal inside the Vatican where he stored stacks of armor and weapons.

When the time was right, Urban VIII started a war to capture more lands and to expand the lands of his Papal States. He destroyed the city of Castor and captured its lands, but the war was expensive. The Roman people became angry as their taxes grew higher.

So did some of the cardinals, and they plotted to have Urban arrested and imprisoned or killed. The pope discovered their plan in time and managed to break up the plot. But now the end was near. Pope Urban had borrowed so much money for his many projects that he was using over 80% of the entire papal income just to pay the interest on his debts.

When Pope Urban VIII died, enraged crowds of Romans rioted and destroyed his monuments. He was one of the most unpopular popes of all time.

The Catholic Church believes an amazing miracle took place during Pope Urban's reign. A modest priest named Joseph lived in the Italian town of Cupertino. He was thought to have a mental handicap, and he often had vivid and exciting religious visions that left him stunned. It was also said that he could float in the air.

His first reported flight took place on October 4, 1630. Apparently Joseph was assisting in a church procession when he suddenly flew up into the sky, where he floated over the crowd. When he came back down he was so embarrassed that he ran to his mother's house and hid. This was his first flight, but not his last.

Joseph's most famous flight allegedly occurred while he went meet Pope Urban VIII. He bent down to kiss the Pope's feet and suddenly floated up into the air. It is said that he continued to have ecstatic fits and to fly in the air until his last mass in 1663, where his final flight was supposed to have been witnessed by thousands of people.

In 1763 the Pope Pius VI canonized him as Saint Joseph of Cupertino. 'The Flying Saint' is the patron saint of pilots and airline passengers, and also of people with mental handicaps.

Figure 22 - Joseph of Cupertino; 'The Flying Saint'

POPE CLEMENT XIV (1769-1774)

Giovanni Ganganelli was crowned Pope Clement XIV after an election heavily influenced by the Holy Roman Emperor and the King of France. The huge debts of the church had finally been reduced, but the popes had lost most of their influence over the kings of Europe.

Pope Clement took over as pope at a difficult time. An earlier pope had led the papal army into a massive defeat that ended with a humiliating surrender to Austria. Then the pope who ruled before Clement had outraged all the kings of Europe by claiming to have the power to annul their laws.

France had occupied the papal lands in France, and the King of Naples had seized lands from the Italian Papal States. Clement IV had been the preferred candidate of the King of France, which meant he was not popular with the other kings.

Pope Clement's priority was to improve his relationship with the Catholic kings of Europe. He was successful in negotiating the return of some lost papal lands. In return he caved in to royal pressure and agreed to suppress the Jesuits, an order of priests who thought of themselves as 'God's Soldiers'.

The Jesuits' single-minded devotion to the teachings of the church often led them into conflict with laws made by kings. They were widely believed to form plots against Catholic monarchs who they believed were drifting away from the true faith, and they were ferocious in their opposition to Protestants.

The Jesuits had already been banned from several European kingdoms including France and Spain. Those kings confiscated considerable wealth from the Jesuits in their countries. The Jesuits were now crushed in all parts of Europe except Prussia.

The Jesuits were extremely active overseas, setting up missions to convert and teach the native peoples there. This work often interfered with the expansion plans of European colonies in the newly discovered lands. Now the Jesuits were expelled from many of them.

The pope's attempts to appease the European monarchs only seemed to make them increase their demands. Pope Clement stopped meeting with Jesuit leaders, and began to treat them harshly.

The humiliating weakness of the pope's influence over Europe's kings was now obvious to everyone. Pope Clement was openly despised by Catholics who believed the pope should have power over all men, including the kings. The pope was widely seen as little more than a ceremonial figurehead with no real power.

After suppressing the Jesuits Pope Clement XIV suddenly became ill and died. Many people believed he had been poisoned.

POPE PIUS VI (1775-1799)

Giovanni Braschi won a close papal election as a compromise candidate. He was nobody's favorite choice, but nobody was greatly opposed to him. He had once been married, and was described as a charming aristocrat. After he promised not to re-establish the Jesuits, he was crowned as Pope Pius VI.

In the beginning he was a reformer who cracked down on corruption in the church and the Papal States. He cut expenses and encouraged agriculture in the Papal States. Unlike most popes, Pius VI did not set out to enrich his own family.

Pope Pius was also a vain man. He was a tall, handsome man who was very proud of what he called his "elegant legs." He had his name carved all over the city, often in letters six feet high. Pius borrowed money to build large monuments in Rome that looked a lot like ancient Egyptian obelisks. The people of Rome began to make jokes about him.

The wild-spending King of France had completely run out of money. He called a meeting of the 'three estates' to see if they would help him raise more money. For centuries Europe's social system had been divided into three classes of people: 'those that fight' (the nobles), 'those that pray' (the clergy), and 'those that work' (the peasants).

Peasants made up over 90% of the population. In recent years some peasants had become merchants and made their livings buying and selling goods instead of working in agriculture. This 'middle class' has accumulated significant wealth, and that is why the French king had called a meeting of all three estates to discuss ways to solve his financial crisis.

Many of the French priests lived in deep poverty while their bishops lived like rich aristocrats. When the clergy and the common people would not agree to give more money to the nobles, the French revolution began.

The revolutionary government in France ended the taking of religious vows. Before the revolution if a priest or nun left the church they were became an outlaw. Now there was a mass exodus from the church. At the monastery in Cluny for instance, 38 of the 40 monks who lived there quit and walked away.

At first Pope Pius remained silent, fearing the French might form their own national church. But payment of tithes to the church stopped, and then church property was confiscated and sold. All the other kings of Europe feared their own people might revolt, so they declared war on France. Pope Pius then condemned the new French republic for upsetting the sacred and divine social order.

Thousands of clergy left France, and the new French government took over matters like registering marriages and births. They also legalized divorce. France became a secular state with no official religion.

The armies of Europe's kings attacked France from all sides. To everyone's surprise, they were all defeated and driven back by the French army led by Napoleon Bonaparte. Napoleon invaded Italy and quickly captured the richest parts of the Papal States, then he threatened to capture Rome.

Pius VI made peace with Napoleon, but he had to hand over millions in gold as well as priceless art works and ancient manuscripts. Napoleon later took over the rest of Italy and made the pope pay a second ransom to prevent Rome itself from being conquered. It made little difference. A French general was murdered while he was visiting Rome, and as a result the French army marched into the city without opposition from the Romans.

Pope Pius VI escaped, moving from city to city as an exile until he died a year later in 1799. He had one of the longest reigns of any pope.

POPE PIUS VII (1800-1823)

Luigi Barnaba Chiaramonti had been promoted to cardinal after one of his relatives became Pope Pius VI. That is probably why Luigi took the name Pius VII when he was elected pope. When he was crowned, he wore a tiara made of paper because the French had plundered the jeweled tiara along with other church property.

When the French army had invaded Italy, Pope Pius said the Catholic religion was not against democracy, and that Christ himself had preached the equality of man. The new pope established friendly relations with Napoleon, over the objections of many of his cardinals. Pius VII even went to Paris when Napoleon decided to crown himself as an emperor.

Napoleon soon crowned himself as King of Italy too, and his army seized the Papal States. When the pope refused to co-operate, Napoleon's army entered Rome and took Pope Pius prisoner. The pope remained in exile until he agreed to Napoleon's demands.

Pius was taken to Paris to meet with Napoleon, but when he got there Napoleon had already left to lead an invasion of Russia. Napoleon returned that winter, leaving his dying army behind. The pope had no idea that Napoleon had already been defeated, so he signed a paper surrendering all his lands including Rome. The cardinals were shocked, but the pope told them he had no choice. The pope claimed the French had dragged him to the table and forced him to sign.

Napoleon himself was now forced to abdicate, and Pope Pius was able to return to Rome in triumph. It is said that when he entered Rome, thirty young men from Rome's richest families unhitched the horses from his carriage and pulled it themselves through the streets to St Peter's.

The Kings of Europe met at the Congress of Vienna and rewarded the pope's resistance to Napoleon by giving him back almost all his lost lands. Europe was in ruins, and where Napoleon had ruled there were new institutions like civil marriage and divorce, free speech and religious tolerance. None of these things were pleasing to the pope and his cardinals.

Pope Pius was able to negotiate agreements with most of the European kings. Often the church received more than anyone expected. The kings agreed to pay the clergy in their countries, but they insisted on the right to appoint the bishops they were paying.

Pope Pius VII died in 1823 after falling and breaking his thigh. He had outlived his old enemy Napoleon by two years.

POPE LEO XII (1823-1829)

Annibale Genga was very ill when he was crowned as Pope Leo XII. None of the cardinals expected him to live long, but he surprised them all by getting better.

People were exhausted after the revolutionary wars of Napoleon. Everyone longed for peace and stability. This was the beginning of the 'Romantic Age' which viewed the Middle Ages as the good old days when life was simple and predictable. This fit perfectly with Pope Leo's agenda.

He restored old laws, making Latin the language used in the churches and courts of his Papal States. Leo XII also made new rules covering almost every detail of his subjects' lives. For instance, he made it illegal for women to wear tight dresses, and he forbid people to play any games on Sundays.

He forbid Roman bars from selling alcohol, which caused an epidemic of public drunkenness. Some of the pope's representatives in other papal cities went even further. They banned gambling, forbid free speech and imprisoned people without trial.

People became unhappy with all the regulations and threatened to rebel. Pope Leo responded with violence, including torture and executions. He set up a system of spies and encouraged people to denounce their neighbors. The pope also persecuted the Jews, locking them inside walled ghettos and forbidding them to own property. Jews who could afford to do so moved away and took their money with them.

The church controlled the legal system in the Papal States, and the pope used it against people he suspected of having modern ideas. Pope Leo XII and his extremely conservative views became very unpopular. The Papal States had become a harsh police state, and the economy began to collapse.

Leo XII even turned against the King of Spain, Europe's most Catholic country. The pope angered him by sending missionaries to work in Mexico and Columbia while those countries were revolting against Spanish rule.

Lack of money became a serious problem for the pope. He held a Jubilee in Rome, and put all charities under church control. It wasn't enough, and the church was in serious financial trouble by the end of his reign.

Pope Leo XII had tried to return the Papal States to a feudal aristocracy. When he died quite suddenly in 1829, he was ruler of the most backward state in Europe.

POPE GREGORY XVI (1831-1846)

It was a troubled time in Europe when Bartolomeo Cappelarri became Pope Gregory XVI. The French people had revolted and thrown out their king again, and the Spanish were still recovering from their own revolution. The pope Gregory replaced had only reigned for a shore time, and there were rumors he had been poisoned.

The French army was invading Italy, and after the harsh reign of Leo XII, people living in the Papal States were beginning to revolt. Within three weeks of Gregory's election, several of his cities had been taken over by soldiers from the French Republic.

The new pope received help from the Austrian army. Pope Gregory was able to suppress the rebellion and arrested all the rebel leaders who had fought for freedom from church rule. Pope Gregory ordered mass executions and other punishments.

The pope also organized 'volunteer police' forces in his cities to arrest and beat up anyone who protested. Soon the prisons were overflowing, but fighting continued to break out. All over Europe the pope's name became associated with the cruel repression of freedom-loving people.

Pope Gregory formally condemned any person who revolted against their monarch. For centuries the church had worked closely with the Kings to rule the common people. Now many people wanted to be free from this 'alliance of throne and altar'.

Gregory not only opposed reform of the church, he hated modern ideas of any kind. He refused to let people use modern inventions like railroads and street lights in his kingdom. He worried that people might gather under streetlights and plot against him. He was against freedom of the press and against Italian nationalism.

His angry reply to suggestions for church reform was blunt: "It is absurd and supremely insulting to suggest the church stands in need of restoration and regeneration." He published a book upholding the infallibility of the pope.

Pope Gregory needed a lot of money to pay for his armies, policemen, and prisons. He was forced to borrow millions, leaving the church with an enormous debt when he died very suddenly. The cause of death was a sudden attack of erysipelas, a skin infection sometimes called 'holy fire'.

POPE PIUS IX (1846-1878)

Giovanni Ferretti was elected by cardinals who did not want another leader like the extremely harsh Pope Gregory XVI. Giovanni took the name Pius IX.

He was a friendly and simple man, the son of a Count and a Countess, and one of Giovanni's first acts was to release most of the prisoners locked up by Pope Gregory. He also allowed the use of modern inventions within his papal kingdom.

In 1848 revolutions against rule by kings broke out across most of Europe, including Italy. Pius IX was forced to flee from Rome, and he considered moving to Germany. Things settled down and he returned to Rome, but he was no longer sympathetic to new ideas.

He forbid Catholics to vote or to run for office in democratic elections in Italy. He also published a Syllabus of Errors condemning developments in the modern world.

Italian revolutionaries were trying to unite the Italian states into a single nation, and they captured all the pope's territories except Rome, which was now guarded by French troops. The pope felt betrayed. Many of the revolutionaries were men he had set free from prison when he was first elected.

The greatest accomplishment of Pope Pius IX was organizing the First General Council at the Vatican. All 700 bishops were invited to attend, and most of them did. Debates went on and on about which church beliefs were true and which beliefs should be open to question.

In the end a large majority of the bishops voted for a declaration that the pope was infallible and was never wrong when teaching about matters of faith and morals. This so annoyed Prussian Chancellor Bismarck that he declared a 'culture war' against the church. The General Council ended abruptly when France and Prussia went to war in 1870.

The French troops who had been protecting the pope were called home to protect their own country, and the Italian revolutionary army marched into Rome. All that was left to the pope was a 'miniature state' - the offices and palaces around the Vatican in Rome, and one castle in the countryside.

Pope Pius IX declared that he was being held as a prisoner inside the Vatican although he was never actually locked up. He had the longest reign of any pope in history, almost 32 years, and by the time he died in 1878 almost everything in the world around him had changed.

A famous miracle was reported during the reign of Pope Pius IX. The Virgin Mary appeared in front of two children in the mountains of southwestern France.

Soon after there was another sighting not far away near the French town of Lourdes. A fourteen year old peasant girl named Bernadette said she had seen a woman inside a cave who claimed to be 'the immaculate conception'.

The pope had always been fascinated by the Virgin Mary, so these miraculous sightings of her made him very excited. Pius worked hard to build up the cult of Mary and the Immaculate Conception. He later also promoted the cult of the Sacred Heart. Pictures of the Virgin Mary, and of Pope Pius IX, became common in Catholic homes around the world.

According to the church, miracles are divine events that have no natural or scientific explanation. For instance, in order to be officially declared a Saint you must do more than lead a virtuous life of good deeds to others. You also need proof that you have performed at least two miracles. In recent years science has been able to explain many things that would have been considered miracles in the past.

Today the vast majority of reported miracles involve very ill people who prayed and then got better for reasons the doctors cannot explain. The Vatican appoints a Miracle Commission which considers the evidence and give the pope their opinion. Only God can make a saint, but the pope must confirm what God has done.

A shrine was built near Lourdes at the site where young Bernadette claimed a "small young lady" had appeared to her 18 times in 1858. By 1859 thousands of pilgrims were visiting Lourdes; it became one of the world's leading Catholic shrines and the number of visitors grows each year. In 1933 Pope Pius XI made Bernadette a saint.

Figure 23 – Thousands of Pilgrims and Tourists visiting Lourdes

POPE PIUS X (1903-1914)

Giuseppe Sarto was elected pope in 1903 and took the name Pius X. He was one of the rare popes who did not come from a wealthy family; he was the son of a mailman. He has been called 'the first peasant pope in 300 years'. He was a warm, friendly man but he held a deep hatred for modern ideas. He once said modernism was "the synthesis of all heresies".

The new pope had worked at the parish level for years among the common people, and he began to make the church more effective at the local level. He simplified the canon of church laws and introduced a simple catechism for everyone to use. He told his priests to teach in the language people used instead of Latin.

He also urged people to attend communion more often. He changed the age of first communion from fourteen to seven. Finely dressed little children made Sundays at church feel more like a family celebration.

Pope Pius liked the common people to be active in the church but not in politics. He said the duty of the people was "to carry out in a submissive spirit the orders of those in control." He particularly disliked socialism and liberalism, and thought that scholarly investigations into the facts about early Christianity were "heresy and betrayal".

The pope condemned France for its religious tolerance and supported Catholic minorities in Ireland in their fight against England. Pius X even refused to meet with American President Roosevelt because the president was also going to meet with Protestants while he was visiting Rome.

New discoveries in science and history were a real problem for the church. It was hard to reconcile some of the bible stories and church teachings with discoveries like the true age of the earth and the theory of evolution.

Pius tried hard to suppress new knowledge. He set up a secret society to spy on teachers and scholars who were investigating new ideas. Even bishops and cardinals were spied upon. Some teachers say this network of spies and organized harassment set church scholarship back fifty years.

Although Pope Pius X fought stubbornly against scientific discoveries and modern inventions, he was at heart a simple man. He often said: "I was born poor, I have lived poor, and I wish to die poor." The eruption of World War One in Europe upset the pope, and may have contributed to his death in August 1914. He was canonized as a saint in 1954.

POPE PIUS XI (1922-1939)

When Ambrogio Ratti was elected pope in 1922 he took the name Pius XI. He had worked as a priest and librarian, then was promoted to Archbishop and sent on a diplomatic mission to Poland.

While he was in Warsaw in 1920 the city was besieged by invading Russian communists. He was the only western diplomat who refused to flee. For the rest of his life he considered communism the greatest danger facing the church.

The previous pope, Benedict XV, had been careful to remain neutral during World War One. He was so successful that each side accused him of favoring the other. Most of the old European monarchies collapsed during the war. The situation in Europe was now dangerously unstable.

Pius XI began making treaty agreements to ensure the rights of the church within the countries of Europe. He became the first international leader to sign a treaty with Adolph Hitler, leader of the newly elected Nazi government in Germany.

Unlike previous popes, Pius XI proclaimed that the church "is not bound to one form of government more than to another, provided the Divine rights of God and of Christian consciences are safe." He warned against the excesses of both socialism and capitalism. Pope Pius was the first pope to use radio to broadcast his messages around the world.

The pope's greatest diplomatic success was an agreement he signed with Mussolini, the fascist dictator of Italy. The Vatican became an independent city-state (the smallest nation in the world) with the Pope Pius as its head of state. Mussolini also paid the pope a huge sum of money to compensate for all the Italian property seized from the church in the past. At a time when the world economy had collapsed into a terrible depression, the pope was suddenly rich.

At first Pius XI applauded Mussolini as "a man sent by providence", but relations got steadily worse. Pope Pius did not condemn Italy's invasion of Ethiopia, but he did condemn the teaching of racial hatred and the persecution of Jews in Italy and Germany.

The Nazi party now took control of all education and youth organizations in Germany. They interfered with the church's activities and arrested any clergy who protested. The Pope was outraged, but he received little support from the frightened democracies of Europe. Nobody wanted to start another war so soon after World War One had ended.

Pope Pius accused them all of "a conspiracy of silence" against the church. In 1938 the pope called the Nazi a cult that was replacing the true God with a national religion based on racial superiority. When the pope died of a heart attack in 1939, the Catholic Church had moved closer to the liberal views of most democratic nations. But World War Two was about to begin, and the pope that came after Pius XI would take a very different view.

POPE PIUS XII **(1939-1958)**

Eugenio Pacelli was crowned Pope Pius XII in 1939 just as the nations of Europe prepared for another war. Pius XII had spent many years as the former pope's representative in Germany. Pius XII loved German music and culture. He even used German to speak with his household staff in the Vatican.

He was the man who had negotiated a treaty between the Vatican and Nazi Germany when Hitler was first elected; it became the first international treaty any government signed with Hitler. When World War Two began he struggled to remain neutral.

Pope Pius XII believed the previous pope had been wrong to keep attacking Germany for spreading racial hatred. Pope Pius admired the unity and strong leadership in Germany, and he believed the church should try to be friends with both sides in the coming war. Before long people began calling him 'Hitler's Pope'.

Pope Pius was convinced that the true enemy of the church was "Godless communism". At the beginning of the war his policy had only two aims: to crush communism and to preserve the church. His focus was always on the fight against the communists, not the fight against the Nazis.

His opinion slowly shifted as the Vatican received more and more reports from its churches all over Europe describing Nazi atrocities, particularly against Jews. Twelve million Jews were sent to slave labor camps.

Six million Jews, including one million children, were murdered by the Nazi.

The pope remained silent.

When Hitler's armies marched into Rome, Pius did allow thousands of Roman Jews to take refuge inside the Vatican. He also acted as a go-between in a failed plot to assassinate Hitler, although privately he worried about the morality of his involvement. At the same time, he condemned leaders of the Allies for insisting that Germany surrender unconditionally.

When the war had definitely turned against Germany, the pope finally spoke out against the Nazi campaign of racial hatred and murder. As the war ended, Pius XII used the Vatican's power and money to help some of the millions of displaced people who had lost their homes and property.

Although Pius XII might not have known about it, the Vatican also became an escape route used by many war criminals fleeing Europe for the safety of South America. After the war ended many people felt the pope had lost his moral credibility by not actively opposing the Nazi.

Pope Pius now launched an attack on the spread of modern ideas in the church. He forbid many distinguished theologians to teach or to publish their beliefs.

Pope Pius XII had been a huge admirer of the Virgin Mary since he was a boy. He used his powers as the pope to promote the cult of the Immaculate Heart of Mary, and in 1950 he defined the dogma of the Assumption of Mary. Although unsupported by scripture and unknown to the early church, Pope Pius invoked his power of 'magisterial infallibility' to define the doctrine of the Assumption.

The pope became gravely ill in 1954, the same year he made Pope Pius X a saint and sent his body on tour in a glass coffin. Pope Pius XII's illness slowly worsened until he died in great pain in October, 1958.

During the pope's years of sickness he suffered from hallucinations and nightmares, and it is said his "blood-curdling screams could be heard throughout the papal apartments."

As a gruesome postscript to his death, the embalming went horribly wrong. The body of Pope Pius decomposed so rapidly that the traditional viewing of the body by the faithful had to be suddenly ended because people were getting sick to their stomachs.

POPE JOHN PAUL I (1978)

Albino Luciani became Pope John Paul in August 1978. The pope was a modest and cheerful man who wanted to help the poor. Unfortunately, he was never given a chance. He died under rather mysterious circumstances just 33 days after he became pope.

The Vatican's official report of his death said the Pope died of sudden heart attack while reading in bed. Rumours of murder began to spread when it was revealed the Vatican had not told the truth about how the body was discovered. The rumours grew louder when the Vatican refused to allow an autopsy on the pope's body.

There were also problems with the death certificate, and there were different versions given of what the pope had been reading when he died. A persistent story said when he died he was holding a document which revealed mafia connections to the secretive Vatican Bank.

The Vatican Bank's official name is The Institute for Religious Works. It is located inside the pope's palace, with an elevator connecting it to the popes' bedrooms upstairs. Since the Vatican is treated as an independent country, the bank can operate in complete secrecy and nobody outside the bank really knows what happens there. It is known that some very wealthy Italians have private accounts in the bank where they can hide their money to avoid paying taxes, or to hide the sources of their income.

The bank has been caught laundering money, and some of that money has been linked to the mafia. There is widespread suspicion the Vatican Bank is involved in a lot of corruption and fraud, but since the bank polices itself, it is very difficult to prove anything.

Under pressure from European bank regulators, the Vatican bank released its first financial report in October 2013. The bank is rich with money from Sunday collections and charitable giving. It revealed assets worth seven billion dollars.

Over a billion dollars is held in cash, often a sign of money-laundering. Unidentified account holders use agents to make deposits and withdrawals; the account owner's true identity doesn't appear to be recorded at the bank. Vatican Bank officials had already been linked to a huge bank failure in Italy that involved the mafia and murder. There were also allegations that the Vatican Bank was connected with the mafia in a fraud involving counterfeit stock and bond certificates.

In 2013 Nunzio Scarono, a senior member of the Vatican was arrested for trying to smuggle twenty million Euros into Italy from a Swiss bank account. His nickname was

'Monsignor 500' because he liked to keep his pockets full of 500 Euro bills (each bill worth over 600 dollars). In 2014 he was also charged with laundering money using fake donations to the church.

Soon after Pope Francis was elected in 2013 he started an investigation into the Vatican Bank's operations. The bank's top two managers suddenly resigned. The results of the investigation appear to have shocked Pope Francis. In January 2014 he fired four of the five cardinals overseeing the bank.

Was the sudden death of Pope John Paul connected to corruption at the Vatican Bank? Is there truth to the persistent rumours that he was killed because he was about to expose and eliminate the bank's criminal connections? Convincing evidence of foul play has never been produced, but lingering doubts remain.

POPE BENEDICT XVI (2005-2013)

Joseph Ratzinger grew up in Germany during World War Two, where he was a member of the Hitler Youth and served in the army. After the war he became a professor and was made a cardinal in 1977. He spent over twenty years directing the *Congregation for the Doctrine of Faith* (formerly known as the *Roman and Universal Inquisition)*. Then in 2005 Cardinal Ratzinger was elected pope and took the name Benedict XVI.

He offended Jews by lifting the excommunication of Bishop Williamson, a notorious Holocaust denier. He also offended Muslims, saying: ""Show me what Muhammad brought that was new and there you will find things only evil and inhuman."

In 2012 the pope's private butler was arrested for giving some of Pope Benedict's private letters to the press. The scandalous letters revealed infighting and corruption among the pope's own staff at the Vatican. The butler said he did it to fight 'evil and corruption' in the church. He was sentenced to prison and locked up, although the pope later pardoned him.

Pope Benedict XVI set the record for making new saints; he canonized 45 new saints during his seven year reign, more than all the popes in the past five hundred years put together. The Catholic Church does a formal investigation to determine if someone is eligible for sainthood, and the cost of an investigation can cost hundreds of thousands of dollars. Some Catholics complain about using so much church money for this purpose.

Pope Benedict XVI also had to defend the Vatican Bank against accusations of money laundering after a priest was caught helping the mafia launder money they made from their criminal activities.

Benedict XVI was outspokenly opposed to contraception, divorce, and homosexuality. When the Anglican Church allowed women to be ordained, Pope Benedict responded by making the ordination of women in the Catholic Church a grave edict under church law, putting it in the same class of church crimes as child abuse.

Pope Benedict's reign coincided with a huge sex abuse scandal that has rocked the Catholic Church around the world. Thousands of priests are accused of abusing children, and church leaders are accused of hiding this abuse. When a priest was caught or confessed, the church dealt with him secretly, usually by transferring him to a new location. In his position as head of the Inquisition for 24 years, Pope Benedict had detailed knowledge of sexual abuse of children.

Benedict confirmed the rules of confidentiality that protected priests and allowed so much abuse to be covered up for so long. The church uses its own courts and did not report abusive priests to the police until 2010. When priests were accused, most were never charged with crimes because the church refused to release their evidence to the local police.

Pope Benedict himself was named in a lawsuit for his role in covering up child abuse. Rather than defend himself, he claimed diplomatic immunity from prosecution because the Vatican is an independent nation. The Catholic Church continues to pay millions of dollars each year to settle pedophile lawsuits. By 2011 over 25 million Catholics in the USA said they were no longer practicing their faith.

A United Nations human rights committee later declared that the Vatican had "systematically" adopted policies that allowed priests to rape and molest tens of thousands of children over decades. They urged the church to open its files on pedophiles and to expose the bishops who concealed their crimes. The committee said the Vatican "has consistently placed the preservation of the reputation of the church and the protection of the perpetrators above the best interests of the abused children.

In early 2013 Pope Benedict XVI resigned from the papacy, the first pope to voluntarily give up his position in almost 500 years. He blamed the physical and mental demands of the job. He now lives in a newly renovated monastery in the Vatican gardens where he devotes himself to a life of prayer.

Figure 25 - Pope Benedict XVI, 'God's Rottweiler'

THE GREAT POPES

There have been some truly great popes in the past. Pope Leo the Great reigned in the fifth century and established the church in Rome as the supreme authority for settling disputes between other churches. In the sixth century, Pope Gregory the Great told the clergy to provide care for the people by setting a good example of Christian behavior. He said the pope should be "the servant of the servants of God".

In the twentieth century, Pope John XXIII stands out as a man who was truly kind and wise. Pope John was already 77 years-old when he became pope in 1958. In Rome he visited hospitals and convalescent homes; at Christmas he visited prisons. Pope John spoke of updating the church, and said: "I want to open the windows and let some fresh air in".

Pope John XXIII wrote an encyclical entitled 'Peace on Earth'. He told Catholics that both human rights and human responsibilities need to be recognized as the foundation for world peace. Even the communists applauded the pope's initiatives toward world peace.

Pope John opened the Second Vatican Council in October 1962, welcoming over two thousand delegates and visitors from all over the world to discuss the role of the Catholic Church and the modern world. He said the church must recognize the authentic faith and goodness of non-Catholics and non-Christians. The whole world mourned when Pope XXII died on June 3, 1963.

Pope John Paul II was elected in 1978. He came from Poland, the first non-Italian to become pope since 1522. He travelled far more than any previous pope; by the middle of 1997 the pope had visited over one hundred different countries and had become a media sensation. In church matters he was very conservative, but in public he spoke of social justice and restored the pope's status as the spiritual center of the church.

He returned to his homeland seven times, and Poland became the center of protests that eventually brought an end to communist rule in Eastern Europe. The pope gave church money to the protesters, and also worked closely with American President Reagan. Russian President Gorbachev later said that without the work of Pope Paul II, the Berlin Wall would never have fallen.

Pope Francis was elected in March 2013. The Catholic Church was at a very low point when Pope Benedict XVI suddenly retired. The church was being rocked by a horrible child abuse scandal and by criminal investigations into the Vatican Bank. The new pope faced terrific challenges.

Francis is the first pope from the Americas. He worked among the poor as a priest and Archbishop in Argentina, and when he became Pope Francis he refused to live in the papal palace. Pope Francis has acted quickly to clean up corruption the Vatican Bank, and he has promised to help victims of child abuse and punish those responsible.

Unlike many popes in the past, Pope Francis appears to be a truly humble and honest man who models the behavior he preaches. So far, Francis has given Catholics hope that he will be able to lead the church through these troubled times. The future of the Catholic Church may depend upon Pope Francis becoming one of the truly great popes.

Figure 26 - Pope Francis; A New Direction for the Catholic Church?

GLOSSARY:

Antipope - someone who claims to be the pope but is not accepted by the church as the true pope

Basilica - a large and important church

Cardinal – a man personally chosen by the pope as an advisor; cardinals vote in elections for new popes

Conclave - a meeting of cardinals to elect a new pope

Council - a meeting of church leaders

Curia - workers who provide administrative support services to a pope or to a bishop

Diocese - the group of Christians living inside the boundaries of an area managed by a bishop

Doctrine - a teaching of the church which is not infallible

Dogma - an infallible teaching of the church which comes directly from the pope

Excommunication - punishing someone by forbidding them to participate in church sacraments and ministries

Heresy - denying the truth of church dogma

Indulgence - cancelling punishment for sins that have been forgiven; selling them for cash led to the Protestant reformation

Infallible - impossibility of being wrong; the pope is infallible when he speaks about faith and morals

Inquisition - a church organization to find and punish heresy, sometimes using torture and execution

Lateran Basilica - the pope's home cathedral and therefore the most important church in the world

Papal States - parts of Italy and France once ruled by the pope as his kingdom

Pope - Italian word for father, used as the title for the head of the Catholic Church

Simony - buying and selling church offices

Sistine Chapel - main chapel for the Vatican Palace where the pope traditionally lives

Synod - meeting of church leaders to talk about the life and mission of the church

CARDINAL, APPLIED TO ANY PRIEST ATTACHED TO A CHURCH

BISHOP, HIGHEST ORDER OF MINISTER IN THE CHURCH.

SELECTED REFERENCES:

Lives of the Pontiffs: The Pontiffs from St. Peter to John Paul II, by Richard P. McBrien

Saints and Sinners: A History of the Popes, by Eamon Duffy

The Catholic Church: A Short History, by Hans Kung

Mortal Sins: Sex, Crime, and the Era of Catholic Scandal, by Michael D'Antonio

Christianity: The First Thousand Years, by Diarmaid MacCulloch

The Case of the Pope: Vatican Accountability for Human Rights Abuse, by Geoffrey Robertson

Render Unto Rome: The Secret Life of Money in the Catholic Church, by Jason Berry

Absolute Monarchs: A History of the Papacy, by John Julius Norwich

Heirs of the Fishermen: Behind the Scenes of Papal Death and Succession, by John-Peter Pham

IF you enjoyed this book,

THEN you might enjoy my next book. My working title is: The End of the Beginning!

The book explores how advances in science and technology are fulfilling bible prophecy.

The merger of religion and science is not only possible, it now appears inevitable. The singularity is coming much sooner than people realize…

Thank you for taking the time to read Sex, Violence and the Popes.

Pat Munro, August 2014

CPSIA information can be obtained
at www.ICGtesting.com
Printed in the USA
LVOW10s1604310717
543272LV00041B/2024/P